Flight of the Raven

Creative Astrology

Shula Slonims

with

Mary Healion-Shelley

AUBURN HOUSE

Published in 1996 by
Auburn House,
An imprint of Salmon Publishing Ltd,
Cliffs of Moher, Liscannor, Co. Clare

The moral right of the author has been asserted.

A catalogue record for this book is available from the British Library.

ISBN 1 897648 66 9

Cover illustration by Shula Slonims
Cover design by Estresso
Set by Siobhán Hutson in Palatino
Printed by Colour Books, Baldoyle Industrial Estate, Dublin 13

For my spiritual guide, Shri P. Rajagopalachari,
my daughter, Rhiannon Kathleen Craven,
my son, Nicholas John Craven,
my mother, Thelma Milton
and my goddaughter, Ayesha Cats

ACKNOWLEDGEMENTS

I wish to thank Mary Healion-Shelley for her insightful editing and support; my dear friend Kirsten Hocking, who insisted on undertaking the daunting task of transcribing the original tapes into a manuscript; David Hill for his inspiration; Jessie Lendennie for more than I can put on one page, and the many people who have shown unfailing love and encouragement, especially my lovely Rachel and Chris.

CONTENTS

THE RAVEN

Then I felt like some watcher of the skies
When a new planet swims into his ken
John Keats 1795-1821

Our family moved from the city of London to the small medieval market town of Rye, in Sussex, when I was about seven years old.

This considerable change, from living on the water in a Thames houseboat to a home on dry land, many miles away, would possibly have unsettled another child. It had no affect on me. There were no real friends to leave behind, no ties to London and, besides, I was more interested in what lay ahead.

Our new home, though tiny by any standards, had none of the confines of a boat and therefore seemed enormous to us children. We had a back garden to play in, a river behind the house where we could watch fishing boats chug past and, directly opposite us, an old castle on a hill. Although I happily shared a bedroom with my sister who is two years older and played with my four year old brother, I was, within myself, a solitary soul. From when I was about three I was aware of being different – a small solemn adult in an overweight child's body.

Now that I understand planetary influences it is obvious why I was such an introspective loner. At the time of my birth three of the major planets, Jupiter, Saturn, and Neptune, were in retrograde, indicating a strong tendency to turn inwards, to explore the internal universe, rather

1

than to look outwards into the world for knowledge.

After the move I made no effort to befriend the local children of my own age knowing very well, through instinct, that we would have nothing in common. Instead I thoroughly enjoyed a solitary nature that peacefully provided an abundance of time and space to observe and think without interruption.

School presented some difficulties. Being shortsighted I could not see the blackboard properly. Boredom and frustration exacerbated my problems although I did teach myself to spell phonetically. Nobody ever explained to me *why* we needed to learn about all that stuff – like geography – or how it might come in useful in later life. Finally I simply switched off to everything except art and focused instead on my internal world,

However, on those occasions when it was necessary to relate to the world outside myself, I was unsure of how I came across to others. Could other people see my weaknesses and vulnerability? I wondered. On realising they could not I simply decided most people were stupid and began to develop a superior attitude to everyone and everything. On reflection this was possibly to protect myself and conceal my problems. Growing up somewhere between dyslexia and illiteracy certainly kept me alert as, every day in one situation or another, I had to do some fast thinking to guard this secret.

About a year after our family settled in Rye I had a unique experience that is, even now, still influencing my life. It was my first real experience of being opened up to the wonders of this world.

A large wild raven appeared 'out of the blue' and

2

descended on the town where it took to frightening people going about their business. It dropped from the sky without warning and relentlessly tried to perch on heads or shoulders. Frightened pedestrians who attempted to repel the creature were rewarded with a vicious pecking on the head. Finally it got to the stage where the authorities were asked to intervene. They succeeded in trapping the bird and sent it off to somewhere in the country. I was not aware of all this at the time.

The raven could not have been sent very far because, in spite of official banishment, it swiftly found its way back to Rye and, once again, began to annoy people.

Then, one unsuspecting day, it found our school. Without warning the huge bird repeatedly swooped at children in the playground and in minutes the area was filled with pandemonium and hysteria. The bird must have been thoroughly enjoying itself for it returned several times.

True to form I generally spent breaks alone, strolling around the play area, chewing grass, watching the other children at their games, making daisy chains or simply enjoying my own private world. I remember dispassionately watching some of these attacks from the sidelines while continuing to feel as totally removed from this excitement as I felt about almost everything else.

Then the great black bird decided to single me out. My initial reaction, as it landed on my shoulder, was no more than amazement at the weight. It was a great deal heavier than I would have expected – had I even bothered to consider such a possibility. Although the raven took me by surprise I was not in the least concerned or afraid.

3

Having grown up with the usual household pets like guinea pigs, a rabbit, and a cat, I had a certain affinity with tame animals. But this was the first wild creature I had ever encountered.

My enduring memory is of feeling honoured to be singled out by this wonderful creature and of fascination with its courage and strong personality.

A careful sidelong glance – I was intent on not upsetting it – revealed the detail and beauty of the raven's feathers. These were not just black, as they seemed from a distance, but rather a shimmering green-blue with purple lights. The large glistening eye, so close to mine, was bold, honest, and unrepentant. It clung to my shoulder, skilfully balanced, as I carefully and slowly walked about the grassy area unaware of everything except my now passive passenger.

The bird stayed only a short time before flying off again and I stood squinting up at it as it disappeared into the vast blue sky. Returning to the classroom, unperturbed and unaware of the other children's awe, I could only think of my shoulder where I still felt the force of its powerful take-off.

The raven came back to the school playground fairly regularly after that and we quickly developed an attachment. Other children who watched it purposefully fly, time after time, directly to my shoulder, decided that the bird and myself were some kind of magical duo. I still did not mix with them or talk about 'my bird' with anyone. Gradually, though, I became pleasantly aware of changes in my attitude towards myself. Now I had begun to consider myself a little bit special.

I looked forward to the raven's visits and soon got to a stage where I was able to recognise 'my bird' at a distance in the sky, through the classroom window, from all other big black birds.

By now word was spreading about the odd relationship we shared and it soon became common knowledge around the town as 'Shula's bird' continued to violently harass people in the streets. I cannot remember my parents discussing any of this at the time so it is quite possible they did not know.

Finally, the Headmaster sent for me. I was invited into his office where he sat me down and gently explained the necessity to capture the raven – pupils and parents were becoming increasingly nervous. This was, he stressed, as much for the creature's own safety as for that of the children and locals. Up until then I had no idea of the havoc it was causing outside the school, that everyone wanted it removed, or, indeed, that I was the only one it had befriended.

He handed me a cardboard carton and asked me to catch the raven and put it into the box. As a child I had no real understanding of loyalty or betrayal. The Headmaster asked and I obeyed.

Even the regional television station became involved. Cameras were in place in the playground and, as the entire school looked on, I was filmed following this notorious bird around. Later, when I saw the news item, all that was apparent was an unidentifiable child's bottom and chubby legs bobbing behind a large black bird which was running along the grass.

Strangely, the raven did not take flight. When it

eventually stood still I bent to pick it up and, for the first time, it lightly pecked my hand as if angry with me. Placing it gently in the box I handed it over to the Headmaster without a word. He told me later that the bird had been sent, with due care and consideration, to the Isle of Wight. It never returned.

The raven's departure left me with a familiar feeling of separateness and isolation that I had all but forgotten in its company. It remained in my thoughts to become little more than an amusing and curious anecdote that I sometimes recounted to various people in a variety of places and situations. Now, looking back, it is as if the creature has always been there to gently encourage me through a series of difficulties towards personal enlightenment.

Not long ago the raven re-surfaced in another form and continues to guide and inspire me. It all began when a friend invited me to dinner at his house in Galway, Ireland, where I now live. David Hill is a professional artist and during the course of the evening, while he was busy in the kitchen, I asked to look through his portfolio.

In the centre of this collection was a picture that completely stunned me. The head and shoulders illustration featured a woman in a mystical setting with a raven on her shoulder. While her hair, colouring, and form were uncannily like my own, the raven perched on her shoulder was exactly as I remembered my feathered friend from childhood. Turning it over I read the details David had written on the back.

'Morrigan. The Morrigan, triple raven-goddess, seducer of enemies, shape-shifter, a powerful force throughout Irish mythology, including the epic *Táin Bo Cuailigne* In many ways the archetypical triadic female deity, The Morrigan often took the form of a raven. Looked upon with awe and suspicion by the ancient Celts.'

I continued to study this picture in wonder, mesmerised by the familiarities of the woman, of her raven, of suddenly being reminded how much my life had improved in the intervening years. And of how these developments have taken me from looking inwards and down as a child to gazing up and outwards as an adult – just as 'my' raven did in our brief time together. Only now, I realised, through years of guided learning, my focus surpasses the sky and reaches further out to the beautiful planets that influence us all and, through them, to our Universe and ultimately, to the Divine.

David's arrival with the food interrupted this reverie. I remarked on how very much I liked the picture of Morrigan and that it reminded me of a childhood incident. I told him about the raven and then finished by joking, 'If I were ever to write my stories, as many people suggested, I would really like you to illustrate them.' Though I am no longer illiterate the idea of seeing my words in print was a completely absurd notion. David accepted the idea with as much levity as I suggested it. The subject was changed from art to food and we did not discuss his work again that evening.

Soon after, he and I were enjoying a stroll along the seafront when we met a friend of his. As we stopped to chat he introduced me to Jessie Lendennie who was walking her dogs.

She invited us for tea at her house and in the course of

conversation I mentioned how much I liked David's work and how one of his pictures unexpectedly reminded me of a childhood experience with a raven. She asked about it and I ended up telling her the story, followed by various others of how a less-than-perfect life had turned around and how I have come to use Astrology as a tool for personal development. At one stage I even laughingly reminded David of his promise to illustrate 'my book'. Jessie suggested I should write it all down, told me she was a publisher, and virtually commissioned this book on the spot. How we would deal with my sparse reading and writing skills, she assured me, would be sorted out later.

The problems were overcome with editorial assistance from Mary Healion-Shelley. Finally, a series of synchronistic steps guided us towards producing this book on spiritually-based Astrology.

I believe, in the roundabout way miracles work, 'my bird' had a significant part to play in all of this – hence the raven on the front cover. But that is not the end of this tale.

Sometime later I went back to David's place and looked through his portfolio again. I found the illustration looking exactly as I remembered – except there was no raven – or any other bird – on Morrigan's shoulder. 'David, this is the same picture of Morrigan, isn't it?' I asked, puzzled. 'The raven I told Jessie about ... where has it gone?'

'Well,' he began, with a quizzical smile, 'I wondered what you meant when I heard you talking about a bird on her shoulder ... there never was one.'

CLIMBING THE MOUNTAIN

*We are all in the gutter but some of us are
looking at the stars.*

Oscar Wilde (1854-1900)

In this book we have the opportunity of examining together, through Astrology, such aspects of spiritual development as The Self (Sun), Receptivity (Moon), The Mind/Consciousness (Mercury), Unconditional Love (Venus), Free Will (Mars), Growth and Expansion (Jupiter), Creating Form and Structure (Saturn), Change and Freedom (Uranus), Surrender (Neptune), Letting Go (Pluto), and more besides.

Anyone who is genuinely interested in reaching a higher level of spiritual awareness will find a personal path. Discovering your own way to begin is rarely a straightforward process and, once found, the journey may not be easy although, as we progress in understanding, we see it need only be as difficult as we choose to make it. There are as many different routes to The Light as there are souls on earth and each must seek its own way. All that is needed to begin is a sincere desire to improve the Self. By consciously acknowledging this fact we set an exciting journey in motion.

My own method of travel is of the 'two steps forwards, one step back,' variety familiar to many. Often uncertain, more than often scary, but always interesting and exciting – like riding a three-legged camel across sand dunes.

Being unable to read until a few years ago I could not

9

find direction through books and some of the people I met along the way were not operating from goodness. Guidance came through instinct and a relentless need to improve myself and therefore my life.

In the process I have learned to love myself and avoid destructive relationships, to give up substances harmful to my body and replace them with goodness like homeopathy, Bach Flower Remedies and spiritually-based group therapies, to reclaim my power, create my own happiness, cry when I feel like crying – and laugh when I want to.

Something as simple as walking in a lovely place, wearing comfortable clothes, or taking a refreshing swim, can remind us of what self love is all about and if we do not love and respect ourself how can we behave like this towards others or expect to improve the direction of this precious lifetime?

Once we decide to change, regardless of where life is at present, the means will manifest in whatever way is suitable for the individual. We all come from different backgrounds, have different experiences and therefore find our spiritual path in different ways. The end result is all that matters.

The journey begins with developing trust in a greater Goodness to guide our steps with Universal love. Learning to love and trust the Self is a fine place to start.

As The Piscean Age fades humankind is becoming less inclined to look 'out there' for help and salvation but is instead adapting to the incoming Age of Aquarius, a time of spiritual focus. We are learning to look within ourselves for answers which, although always in place, we did not previously trust to find there. Humankind has long been conditioned to give away personal power to governments, religion, and other authorities who have, in many instances used it to manipulate. Little wonder there is such resistance from conventional society to New Age ideas.

For many people, all around the world, this era of change is welcomed as a unique opportunity to take charge of their lives and direction of personal and spiritual growth. For others, it is a time of great insecurity – originating in fear from lack of trust.

Change can be difficult for a human to accept yet it continually surrounds us. Nature is forever on the move but we take these cycles for granted.

Day fades into night, spring awakens into summer, autumn drifts into winter. Rain falls, the sun shines, it gets hot and cold, clouds move, moon and tides wax and wane, snow melts, buds open, flowers bloom, leaves drop. No moment of any day is like another. How boring it would be if earthly life were constant; nothing would be born, grow, or die to make room for new life whether it be human, animal, plant, or weather pattern.

That there can be no new direction without change is shown to us every moment of every day and we, as humans, are as much part of nature as any other living thing. It is purely our quest for greater enlightenment that sets us apart.

Experiences from which we can learn will continue to unfold in whatever way is necessary for the individual to develop. The difference is that now we are becoming aware of them as spiritual/evolutionary insights. We have been given these opportunities every day since we were born but it is only through becoming consciously aware they are lessons in development we can begin to grow into our potential.

Whether or not we develop a positive attitude towards whatever changes these experiences will require is purely a matter of personal choice. Some who are unable to move forward become even further entrenched in existing negativity. That is their choice. Free will is forever present.

While some begin by finding the courage to overcome basic human failings such as dishonesty, jealousy or envy, others already attuned to a higher life vibration may only need to surrender to The Light.

One of the most common barriers to moving forward is the tendency to live life as a victim of the past. This can manifest in such ways as unconsciously carrying the limitations of our childhood, family history, past lives, national history, or even the karmic history of the human race.

To try and change this attitude might seem like an impossible task to many but help is at hand from the Source of All Creation and everything can be changed.

It all begins with one positive thought from you. This single thought opens the door to the possibility of change. Once open you are effortlessly welcoming in the potential for transformation and all the goodness life has to offer. When a greater evolved being, such as an Avatar or Spiritual Master, walks through a city the vibration of the entire area is raised by the power of enlightened thought.

My own learning path has been so full of stumbling blocks, pitfalls, and potholes that sometimes I wondered where it was all leading. Having reached a stage of development where I can understand the Divine purpose behind those harsh lessons I am grateful for having experienced what it is like to be different – an outcast – through a variety of cruel, painful, bizarre, and sometimes dangerous situations.

The lessons continue, on a daily basis, throughout our time on this beautiful planet. All we need to do is acknowledge them and look for what is being taught. Once this wisdom is revealed and we accept the teaching by incorporating it into our daily life we need never repeat the same experience.

In order to climb the mountain towards a higher understanding we need to look for ways of opening up to the goodness this life has to offer.

It is appropriate that, as humankind moves into the Astrological Age of Aquarius, we utilise the many aspects of Astrology for effective expansion of personal development to encourage growth and, indeed, evolution. Taking a single step towards finding the Higher Self reveals there are hundreds of methods available by which we can develop in this way. They have always been there. There is nothing new under the sun. We are simply following a basic wisdom that has been carried on through thousands of years although it has been known by many different names.

When most people think of Astrology it is generally to do with 'starry' predictions in newspapers and magazines or even 'Madame Rose' at the seaside or in the teashop.

This book has nothing to do with fortune telling or 'lighthearted stargazing' but rather is intended as a serious means to reconnect head to heart, person to person, to explore the life-force within and all around us. By getting to know the inner self and your relationship with the energies that make up your existence on this planet, you will come to a greater understanding of your part in the cosmos.

Originally Astrology and Astronomy were the same science. The division came over a period of time as more powerful telescopes were invented. Astronomers became astral observers while Astrologers continued to relate the placement of planets to people.

In today's Orient, Astrology retains respect as a science. It is not considered at all odd for large companies to consult Astrologers when making important decisions. This could mean anything from deciding whether or not to do business with another company, what time to schedule a meeting for maximum positive results, or the best position for the public entrance to a new business premises. To many westerners this way of thinking is little more than incomprehensible superstition.

In the old days here in Europe it was not unusual for priests and doctors to consult Astrology to better understand another's problems of a physical or spiritual nature. A good astrologer can be friend, counsellor, and psychologist . However, it must be said that in this, as in any other profession, there are good and bad practitioners. Many are spiritually aware and work with integrity while others are in it simply for greed or other selfish reasons. Choose carefully before consulting.

What then, is the Age of Aquarius? In brief, the Ages gradually occur approximately every 2,200 years as a wobble in the earth's movement gives the precession of the equinoxes.

This movement is backwards through the Zodiac – hence moving from Pisces into Aquarius rather than the other way around. Because the same names exist for the Zodiac and some constellations this sometimes causes friction between Astronomers and Astrologers. The same names do not represent the same celestial area to each group except for a brief time every 25,868 years when the earth completes a full circle and arrives, once again, at the starting point of Aries. Then, for a comparatively short time, the signs of the Zodiac and constellations coincide.

Jesus was born as the Age of Aries (the Ram) passed into the Age of Pisces (the Fish). He was known to his closest disciples as *Ichthys*– the sacred fish – and his original followers were fishermen. So too did the sign of the fish represent early Christianity. However, much of His spiritual teaching was manipulated and corrupted through the generations by those who purported to follow Him. The result was hypocrisy, false piety, self-righteousness and sanctimonious judgement of others. Consider, for instance, the Inquisition, corrupt popes and other clerics, the Crusades, the torture and murder of psychics (and possibly Astrologers!) who spoke the truth, and, of course, the Witch Hunts.

The transition into a New Age is a turbulent time from necessity although according to today's disaster-hungry media that is all that seems to be happening. We see and hear daily evidence of starvation, murder on every scale, drug addiction, sexual horror stories, natural disasters and seemingly inexplicable changes in weather patterns. It is as if our entire planet is plagued with turmoil and chaos in a final rejection of all the old ideas attached to the Piscean Age.

But there is another side. On a positive note the natural balance is also in effect. Just as there is Darkness so too is there Light. Positive changes in place at this moment are moves towards heightened compassion and appreciation of all things.

They include the flowering of our human potential, greater overall sensitivity leading to more respect for the free will of the individual, full awareness of the impact our choices make, and the ability to accept responsibility for our individual and collective actions.

During this evolutionary leap we will also heighten respect for our environment, work diligently on restructuring society to serve rather than enslave, and willingly share ideas and information on an international scale for the benefit of all life. Wider understanding of quantum physics will fuse science with religion through accepting that Light, as in the creative force, is the essence of everything. On a personal level we will courageously accept the limitations of the human condition.

In the Aquarian Age human consciousness will refuse to accept old and ingrained manipulations of Truth and, through rejecting and breaking it down, will expand onto a higher level of spiritual awareness. Everything will be questioned as minds open. Children born now will, unlike previous generations, refuse to accept anything that does not have a basis of honesty and sincerity.

This is a blossoming of humankind. Embrace it and give thanks for being part of the spiritual awakening. Let us now take the first steps towards climbing the mountain together.

RECIPE FOR GROWTH

I feel a recipe is only a theme which an intelligent
cook can play each time with variation.

Madame Benoit

Looking at each of the ten planets individually, at what each symbolises, and how it relates to you, it is possible to see how your own life and the lives of those with whom you come into contact, can be improved.

While learning about Astrology I was often reminded of how I learned to cook. When I got married at sixteen I had no idea how to prepare a meal. My husband Rob taught me with help, inspiration and encouragement, to cook in an intuitive way. With his guidance I progressed to eventually become a professional chef and, at one stage, ran my own vegan cafe.

As an Astrologer I consider the planets as basic ingredients for living in the way organic ingredients come together to make a particular dish. When we decide to prepare a meal one of the first discoveries is that there are different ways to go about it. Initially we study a cookbook and diligently follow the recipe, precisely weighing and measuring as we go. Then, as interest and confidence build, we learn to trust our intuition, eventually becoming adept at this skill. We also discover that two people can follow the same recipe and produce different dishes and that we can achieve subtle differences in flavour when we repeat a recipe ourselves. By realising there are many creative ways of producing a dish we can throw the cookbook away and successfully 'fly solo' – or choose to embrace the challenge of further study to supplement the knowledge we already hold.

In a similar way Astrology provides a recipe for life using the planets as ingredients. Discover how to create a quality of life that is delicious, nourishing and 'easy to digest'.

But what of those who have never learned to cook? Who have no interest in what they eat and could not care less how it is prepared? To them cooking remains a mystery. So too will the skills for an inspired life remain hidden if we cannot be bothered to explore the basic steps. Those who settle for the easy way out and take whatever life offers on a plate may eventually lose respect and appreciation of themselves.

But we must remember that reading the recipe is not the same as eating the meal. Please explore whatever insights this book may offer and leave the rest. It is, like a cookbook, simply a way of introducing ideas that may not have previously occurred. You may choose to follow one of these planetary 'recipes', decide you enjoyed the result, and move on to explore further. Who knows, perhaps you may even come to write your own 'cookbook'. Everything creative is possible.

Each planet has its own unique qualities and properties, many of which we will explore. I have also included a series of exercises with each that have the potential to set personal transformation in action. However, if you are already under guidance from a teacher who has given you specific spiritual practises to follow it may not be appropriate to do these exercises at the same time. Finding a balance is important . Unless you have a good understanding of compatible techniques mixing methods can upset your subtle energy systems and confuse results. Remember, free will is always in place and nobody else is responsible for your personal spiritual development – or your life.

A certain amount of this information is channelled, some is instinctive, more comes from experience. All of it has been tested with positive results.

Perhaps one day we will see a school curriculum include this kind of simple Truth. Had my early education included a basic understanding of how the universe works I would have been so fascinated and stimulated that I cannot imagine having settled for illiteracy. However, in regard to personal growth and development, this difficulty enabled me to learn a great deal more than anything I could have discovered in the classroom.

In order to understand how we can move towards a greater consciousness it is necessary to explore the various states of human existence. All human life exists on each of these levels at the same time:

Physical/Body (Earth), Emotional/Empathic (Water), Intellect/Psychic (Air), Energy/Drive (Fire), Spiritual/Astral (Ether).

While the four basic elements of Earth, Water, Air and Fire have a common place in our everyday lives, the fifth element, Ether, has somehow been separated and ignored by Westerners over the centuries unless in a religious context.

Lack of belief in the existence of this element may indicate humankind's present lack of trust in the Divine aspect of our being. Yet it is this fifth element that links us directly with the Source of all Creation.

The other favourite area of scepticism is whether or not the planets actually have any affect on us. How can they not? Take a brief look at the way our lives are influenced by the Sun. Night dawns into day, with sunlight we become happier, all life grows and flourishes. With the moon's influence all tides, including those within the human body, wax and wane. Moonlight often incites romantic thoughts.

As we examine each planet closely through Astrology the significant effect of each will become more apparent.

THE SUN

There was a roaring of the wind all night;
The rain came heavily and fell in floods;
But now the sun is rising calm and bright

William Wordsworth 1770-1850

Colours: Yellow, Orange, Gold. **Symbol:** The Self.
Energy : Yang.
Rules: Leo. **Mode:** Fixed. **House:** 5th. **Time of Year:**
Midsummer. **Element:** Fire. **Chakra:** Solar Plexus (3rd).
Cycle: 365 days. **Stones:** Ruby, Red Onyx. **Metal:** Gold.
Traditional Association: Father.
Some Herbs and Flowers: California Poppy, Chamomile,
Celandine, Marigold, Rosemary, Peppermint, Rue, Saffron,
Sunflower. **Vegetables:** Avocado, Corn, Squash,
Watercress, Spinach, Rice. **Fruit:** Fig, Orange, Lemon.
Bach Flower Remedies: Heather, Holly, Willow.
Associated Words: Being, Creativity, Day, Determination,
Drama, Ego, Generosity, Heat, Illumination, Individuality,
Life force, Perseverance, Purpose, Radiance, Resource,
Self-expression, Vigour, Vitality.

Earth and the other planets in our Zodiac, except the
Moon, orbit around the Sun which is at the centre of our
Solar System. In Astrology it represents the Life Force, the
sense of Self, our Ego, and provides the opportunity to
explore who we are as a unique part of the Whole. The
Sun does not just shine down on humanity but also
radiates out through us into the world as a vital, open,

spontaneous and natural reminder of Divinity.

To take this opportunity of placing yourself at the centre of your life and viewing the world through your own unique experience it is first necessary to look at the meaning of Ego.

Many people carry a misconception of this word and see it only as representing self-obsession, pride, arrogance and conceit.

It is important to understand there is nothing wrong with the Ego itself. Only our misuse of it causes the problems. Bask in your own light and you will be burnt. Stare at the sun and you will be blinded. Lack of sunlight causes depression – an inability to allow the personal sun to shine within. Proportion is everything. It is as healthy and necessary to have a balanced perception of the Self as it is vital we develop our identity as individuals in order to fulfil our true potential.

When a baby is born it has no sense of Self but rather is more like a receptacle for the attitudes, actions, and atmosphere, to which it is subjected. Mother, the primary source of warmth and sustenance, is a baby's first experience of Sun. As the infant becomes more aware of its surroundings a sense of Self/Ego develops gradually and, within months, grows into its own little 'Sun' with a developing personal solar system as each of the planets begin to noticeably provide other vital aspects of human existence.

Let us take baby's first birthday celebrations as the premier example of Ego development. In the best joyful birthday tradition the infant is personally acknowledged with gifts and/or a party. Family and friends shower it with love, attention, fun, and flattery. Through this extra attention the new Ego is strengthened and supported as the child is recognised as special, a separate being surrounded by love, for no reason other than it exists.

As the child grows to adulthood the need to continue healthy development of the Ego becomes less focused as influence from other planets comes into play. The planets, usually in sequence to their own relationship to the Sun, come into the human consciousness. We gradually develop a personal symbolic solar system, in relation to the planets, through which to journey through all aspects of human consciousness. Everyone has a unique experience of the planets through this process of development according to personal circumstances.

If a child's faults are continually pointed out, before it learns to recognise the Self, low self esteem will easily develop, leading to a belief in the tiny individual that he or she is intrinsically wrong – a state of mind that can negatively influence the remainder of its life. An example of this is when a boy is encouraged to suppress emotions such as fear, confusion or grief. The 'boys don't cry' syndrome. He can become void of natural instinctive reactions and miss out on the understanding gained from expression of these emotions. This sort of suppression limits healthy growth of instinctual wisdom, preventing the adult from striving for the highest aspirations.

From childhood I experienced what it is to deal with low self-esteem through a damaged sense of Self carried through from a past life. It manifested in various ways. At age ten, when I went into hospital to have my tonsils out, I was an obese ten stone. Hospital procedure demanded my weight be checked but I stubbornly refused to have it done in front of anyone and, to accommodate me, the obliging staff pushed the enormous scales into a deserted hall.

At thirteen I suspiciously repelled offers of friendship from a really nice girl. Why would she want a friend who was fat and ugly? I could not see myself as she did because of unflattering pre-conceived ideas rooted in low self-esteem. I went on to indulge in teenage sex with boys I did not particularly like or even know. In early adulthood I came to realise I did not possess the tools to make my life work and began to explore alternative avenues. This quest led me to Astrology and other healing processes.

Once the personal solar system is fully explored we are ready to expand the consciousness to include the Universe and then, with further expansion, encompass the concept of God and the Oneness of Spiritual Light.

The Sun rules the Zodiac sign of Leo, a fire sign, also associated with focusing on the Self. There are various Astrological interpretations on what part of the human body the Sun exerts a major influence.

Some practitioners situate it in the heart and along the spine while others see it centred in the solar plexus. My preference is for the latter as I see the solar plexus as the Ego centre, particularily as the energy of this Chakra is Yang, indicating expressiveness. The Chakras are energy points in the human body of which there are seven major and twenty-one minor. As the Heart Chakra is at the centre it links the lower Chakras to the soul-related higher ones. It is not the self-focused Sun but rather Venus love that links personal to spiritual .

The colours red, orange, yellow, and gold, are traditionally associated with the Sun. If you wish to enhance or lift your mood try surrounding yourself with these colours through clothing, jewellery, or decor in the home.

Bach Flower Remedies are liquid preparations of particular flower essences selected to refine the vibrational energy of the individual. They are prepared according to homeopathic principles, where the dilution is believed to strengthen the potency, and are taken by drops in water. They are available, with extensive information, from complementary or alternative health stores.

Heather helps contact our personal store of vitality rather than draining it from others; Holly improves self-love and therefore assists in loving others; Willow clarifies the giving and taking process.

Ruby is a Yang Sun stone. The vibrations of gemstones subtly resonate in the frequencies of the planets. Through them it is possible to align and balance the energy of the Chakras thus assisting us to learn and integrate the lessons represented by individual planetary energy.

There are many other gemstones, apart from those mentioned here, to which you may become attracted in a sub-conscious need to tune into the Sun's energy or clarify your relationship with your Ego. Consider wearing them as jewellery or simply place them around your home.

All gemstones, as they come into your possession, need to be cleansed of energy from anyone else who may have handled them. This is done by dissolving about a tablespoon of rock salt crystals in a glass of hot water that has previously been boiled for the purpose. Drop your stone into this solution, place the glass on a sunny windowsill for 20 minutes or, alternatively, leave overnight in the dry salt. If touched by someone else it is necessary to go through this purification process again. Maybe it would be best simply to ask friends not to handle or else place them out of reach of curiously admiring hands.

THE SUN RITUAL

Ritual is as old as history and has always been used to evoke a particular energy. Religious ritual takes the form of worship in church, synagogue, mosque, temple or other holy place. The act of daily meditation or prayer is, in itself, a form of ritual. So too, in a secular sense, is laying a table for a celebratory meal, planting a tree in memory of a person or occasion, or preparing the body for anything from physical union with a partner to a medical or surgical procedure.

This Sun Ritual is devised as a conscious creative expression intended to attract a particular spiritual experience for the purpose of higher learning.

In order to evoke experience through any sort of ritual it is vital to continually align yourself with the Divine. Always begin by asking for protection from your personal Source of Universal Goodness, Guides or Guardian Angels.

Find a quiet place where you will not be disturbed. Sit comfortably with your back straight and your hands on your lap, palms upwards, then close your eyes and try to visualise yourself completely bathed in golden sunlight or in the purest white light that originates in the Divine. In your mind's eye imagine this light flowing directly down upon you from the Highest Source and, once it is in place, ask for protection. When you can comfortably achieve this meditative state you are ready to utilise the senses to create and sustain the required atmosphere.

Creating a simple ritual to explore planetary energy is choosing a natural and empowering experience while taking responsibility for the Self. It is a harmless and loving route towards transformation which itself is a gradual process. Expecting instant results or 'blinding flashes' of insight will only lead to disillusionment and disappointment.

Ritual is created by stimulating the senses using colour, scent, sound, movement, thoughts and, if you wish, taste. Choose the Sun's own day, Sunday, for this ritual and the closer to your birthday the better – just before is ideal. It is most important the ritual is performed in whatever way and in whatever place that offers you the most comfort and security.

If you have never experimented with anything like this before why not choose the intimacy of your bathroom for this particular occasion? Add a few fragrant drops of essential oil from one of the Sun's herbs to the bath water as it is running. Avoid Juniper oil if pregnant. Lay out Sun-colour towels and a Sun-scented oil or body lotion to massage later into your freshly-dried skin. Light as many red, orange and/or yellow candles as you like and place them around the room. Place a vase of Sun flowers where you can see them from the bath. Play a pre-prepared tape of gentle 'sunny' music or something warm and soft that you associate with the happiness of summer. This could even be a recording of waves lapping on the beach. As you bask in the surrounding warmth you can, if you wish, enjoy a glass of orange juice, bowl of golden jelly, avocado on toast, or even nibble a fig or two. Enjoy looking at and holding your favourite Sun stone. When the senses are fully aware of all this goodness you can meditate, in this golden light, on your spiritual essence.

Begin by considering who and what you are. It is necessary to establish a picture of the Self before it is possible to improve anything. Do you love and accept yourself as a whole, unique, imperfect part of Universal Goodness? Affirm that you are fine, just as you are, with all the limitations of human life. Accept what you cannot change and acknowledge the potential for improvement.

Ask such questions as what is the purpose of my life? What are my dreams and plans for the future? Do I trust that I have an unending source of vitality from the Sun through the goodness of the Divine ?

All of this may, initially, be easier said than done but practice makes perfect. It is not necessary to get into the bath each time you wish to meditate on the Self in this way. Repeat it at any tranquil opportunity and, if you wish, continue to use the bathroom scenario as a focus to allow your senses to create the same atmosphere. When you are having an ordinary bath allow yourself time, whenever possible, to concentrate on this meditation.

The Sun Ritual is not mere pampering. Only misunderstanding of Ego would claim such non-sense. Look on it as a purification ritual where the Ego is guided by the soul towards a fuller understanding of your potential.

THE SUN EXERCISE

This is a way to get to know yourself better. You will need a pen, paper, an uninterrupted space and plenty of time.

Ask, 'How do I see myself ?'

Now, without pausing to think or compose an answer, immediately begin to write a list. Do it quickly without looking at what you are saying in order to work as much as possible from the subconscious. It is very likely that you will contradict yourself but this is fine as there are many aspects of the Self – logic is only one of them. Write whatever comes to mind and keep going until you naturally come to a halt. It can take a while.

When finished take a short break to change your focus. Return to the list and read aloud what you have written. The effect of hearing your own voice is important as it will increase the impact of your words.

What effect has this had on you? Are your words mainly positive, negative, or a balance of both? It is important not to come to any conclusions or judgement at this time. You may discover some interesting beliefs you hold about yourself. These are important insights into the basic assumptions from which you live your life. Through them you may discover you have been subconsciously limiting self-expression and relationships thereby slowing down your evolution.

It can be beneficial to do an exercise like this without concerning yourself with a final analysis. To simply allow yourself to be all those things and just note your reactions can be enough. If this experience is new to you it may be difficult to concentrate. You may feel sleepy or even be aware of mild physical discomfort. It is surprising how a favourite chair can suddenly become unbearable at a time like this.

Want to go further? A couple of days after completing the first part of this exercise you might like to stand in front of a full-length mirror. Look yourself in the eyes and say aloud, 'I am ... ' followed by the first word on your list and finish the sentence by saying ' ... and that's fine.' Do this slowly and consciously, observing your reactions but not allowing them to interrupt the proceedings until you have completed the list. Emotions might distract you or you may be totally indifferent to the whole thing. 'That's fine'. Simply add your responses to the list.

Take this to yet another stage by replacing the mirror with a good friend or counsellor but remember – no analysis. You are just you, 'and that's fine'.

My list includes; 'spontaneous, honest, lively, a non-smoker, a slow eater, sensual, confident, tired'. What about yours?

THE MOON

And, hand in hand, at the edge of the sand,
They danced by the light of the moon.

Edward Lear 1812-1888

Colour: Silver. **Symbol:** Receptivity. **Energy:** Yin.
Rules: Cancer. **Mode:** Cardinal. **House:** 4th.
Time of Year: late June/July. **Element:** Water.
Chakra: Sacral (2nd). **Cycle:**28 days, **Stones:** Pearl,
Moonstone. **Metal:** Silver.
Traditional Association: Woman.
Some Herbs and Flowers: Borage, Forget-me-not,
Lavender, Lily, Iris, St. John's Wort, Verbena, Geranium,
White Rose, Queen Anne's Lace.
Vegetables: Cucumber, Lettuce, Turnip, White & Red
Cabbage. **Fruit:** Watermelon.
Bach Flower Remedies: Red Chestnut, Chestnut Bud,
Cerato, Crab apple.
Associated Words: Emotion, Past, Receptivity, Night,
Home, Nurture, Mother, Instinct, Protect, Respond, Habit,
Adapt, Astral, Personal, Subconscious, Flow, Roots.

The Moon, although not directly a satellite of the Sun,
revolves around the Earth and both circle the Sun. It
reflects the light of the Sun onto Earth and is noticeably
responsible for daily change in human moods.

Every 28 days the Moon goes through a cycle of New,
First Quarter (waxing), Full, and Last Quarter (waning). It
is best to begin projects at a New Moon and, while it is

32

waxing, to avail of that increasing energy by developing what you have started. Use the Full Moon to accomplish your task and, as lunar power wanes, take this time to reflect.

It is inadvisable to begin a new project of any nature, whether personal or professional, while the Moon is on the wane. Successful farmers and gardeners in various ethnic cultures have traditionally sown, planted and harvested crops, in accordance with lunar phases.

Through its relationship with water the Moon exerts considerable influence on all organic planetary life and in ancient times doctors and priests learned Astrology as a matter of course to better enable them to treat physical and spiritual ills. Many contemporary surgeons are aware that surgery is better avoided at a Full Moon when the patient is inclined to bleed more heavily. As the Moon influences the ebb and flow of tides throughout the world's oceans so too does it influence the cycle of female menstrual fluids.

The Second Chakra, located in the sacral area, is connected with reproduction and the basic human longing to connect and nurture – as a mother does with a child. It also influences emotional bonding, collective consciousness, dreaming and the astral plane.

Nature's lunar-aligned 'jewels' are pearls, symbolising subconscious waters of the emotions, and moonstones which enhance receptivity.

The Bach Flower Remedies associated with the Moon are Red Chestnut, for undue concern and over-protectiveness; Chestnut Bud breaks the cycle of repeating past mistakes; Cerato enhances trust in personal intuition.; Crab Apple dispels unwarranted shame.

In astrology the Moon also symbolises receptivity – a willingness to develop further by raising the consciousness. Those who become too focused on material and physical achievement by basking in personal greatness only shut off the opportunity to learn more. We will always find ways of becoming more spiritually refined through heightened sensitivity if we are receptive.

Not only is it possible to develop a greater awareness of goodness but also to better empathise with the pain and grief of others through exploring our own.

Emotions, linked Astrologically with the Moon and water, sweep in waves and, on occasion, threaten to swamp us.

Tears of joy or sorrow are the moist result of strong emotional experiences and, like all safety valves, are there for a valid reason. Feel free to let them flow – unless those tears are used negatively for manipulation. In this instance it may be necessary to mop up, do some honest evaluation, and seek counselling. Emotional blackmail, in its many subtle or sordid forms, invariably results in pain.

Western society generally disapproves of overt emotional expression and we are taught from childhood to control and even conceal our feelings. This can lead to the mistaken belief that we are controlled by emotions and that, because they are directly linked with the subconscious, they have a life of their own. We quickly learn to hide feelings in order to exert 'control'. Unfortunately such suppression is non-discriminating, making it just as easy to lose pleasurable feelings as well as the painful kind.

The inability to show love is sadly common for all sorts

of reasons. Sometimes parents believe it detrimental to a child's development to regularly show an open display of love; the child might grow up to be a 'big head'. They fear that such a display will diminish parental authority.

Many the hopeful romance is quashed by lovers who take to playing any one of a variety of emotional 'cat and mouse' games.

Husbands and wives can neglect to show affection – or even continue the courtship – once the wedding is over. Perhaps they forget this is a beginning rather than an ending. Newlyweds and not-so-newlyweds might make a point of taking time for regular walks alone together in the Moon's romantic light .

Suppressed emotion leads to a backlog of stored hurt and resentment which in turn may, in extreme cases, manifest in physical or mental illness. When one eventually manages to 'open the floodgates', through whatever means is right for the individual, a lifetime of pain and sorrow pours out.

Sometimes it takes a complete emotional breakdown to release this – by which time professional help and support may be necessary to find the way through a tangle of denial cleverly devised to avoid expressing natural reactions.

When I eventually learned that suppressing emotions did not make them go away I realised it was necessary to make a conscious decision to deal, one by one, with as many individual hurts as I could remember. What followed was like peeling the layers of an onion over a long period of time. Further on in this chapter I have included a Moon Exercise based on weeping to help instigate your 'peeling' process.

I began by arranging to spend time with a trusted friend who willingly agreed to participate. The session involved honestly recounting a hurtful experience in detail to this 'safe' person then allowing myself to cry about it and finally let the pain go. The release was wonderful although this evaporating hurt revealed another underneath and, I soon discovered, the greater the pain, the deeper it is buried. As I got closer to the heart of my personal onion the anguish increased and each layer took more tears to release.

When each emotion arose I noticed that all the old beliefs I had used to suppress it came to the surface also. Thoughts flooded into my mind like, 'This is foolish.' 'My friend does not want to hear this boring stuff.' 'I might get angry.' 'Why bring up the past?' 'If I let go now I'll never be able to compose myself again.' 'I may be in danger if I let my true feelings show.' These beliefs can be released with the old pain.

Most of us have developed an array of conditioned beliefs designed to suppress normal, healthy, and essential reactions to suffering. If we are to improve quality of life it is necessary to change existing patterns and re-learn how to deal with our feelings. We need to affirm it is within our power to secure future safety and that Divine protection is in place.

After exploring my emotive reaction to pain, although it seemed like self-centred indulgence at the time, I was able to honestly forgive myself and others and finally forget some hurts I had been carrying around for years. As the pleasure of unburdening increased I would not have been surprised had I floated up to the Moon the moment the last one, in that session, was released.

However, we cannot expect to be magically immunised against harbouring new hurts. My way of dealing with this is to spend time alone, or with a willing friend, and go through the peeling process again which invariably means a weep. Tears are a symbol of cleansing and purification and no cause for shame. Look on them as a convenient means to wash away hurt. By dealing with pain in this way we are better able to enjoy living in the present moment knowing there is no need to push healthy emotions away in order to 'control' the self.

Value those emotions while reminding yourself they are temporary and rooted in the subconscious. A temporary sense of relief may be found in reacting to others from the emotions although remorse can set in later for what was said or for a given impression. On the other hand, if a backlog of hurt has been cleared and you understand yourself better, a strongly emotive situation can be turned into a learning process. When a person or situation triggers strong feelings try to find clues as to what is really happening. Are they, for instance, being sparked by a previous association? Is it appropriate to react at all? Ask what your natural feelings are.

No reference to aspects of the Moon would be complete without looking at the fascinating business of dreams and astral travel.

Everyone dreams – although some block them out or simply do not remember. There are different categories of dreams and all can be recorded by consciously determining to do so before going to sleep. Be patient, this may take a little practise. Placing a pad and pen or tape recorder by your bedside will help.

Some dreams are a release of images and clearing of impressions from the day. Others are symbolic, coming as messages from the Higher Self, to help us understand what is happening on a spiritual level. Lucid dreaming is, like deep meditation, where one is conscious in a dream state and it is possible, through practise, to use this experience to change, direct, or enhance life. In lucid dreams we are introduced to a freedom familiar to the spirit but unknown on the physical plane. In this state we have the power to be anything we want and it is possible to gain amazing insight into subconscious desires.

Astral travel is not actual dreaming but rather an 'out of body' experience where the spirit soars without boundaries. I have had many personal experiences of two particular kinds of astral travel. The first, where I am called out to help another, and secondly, where I consciously choose to leave the body. There are no symbolic images in the astral plane such as in dreams but rather a full consciousness. Astral travel is sometimes mistaken for dreaming by those who are not aware of having experienced it.

THE MOON RITUAL

This is devised to facilitate emotional release and while the ideal time to do it is at night at a Full Moon, when the internal emotional tides are at their highest, it can also be done privately at any time when the need arises. The intention is for you to cry and let go of hurt which may not be as simple to instigate as it initially seems.

First arrange a time where you will not be interrupted and choose a comfortable place such as in your bed, bath or comfortable chair. Prepare the area by placing a box of tissues within reach and lighting a candle. If possible use a silver coloured holder with a silver, white or dark blue candle. For additional atmosphere add a couple of drops of Lavender oil to a bowl of hot water and set it beside the candle.

Turn on a lengthy tape of gentle instrumental music at low volume. Close your eyes, relax, take several deep breaths, and ask for spiritual protection. Encourage your mind to drift, reminding yourself this is a positive opportunity to release emotional pain. Through making the physical preparations your intention is already in place.

Allow yourself to naturally focus on your most conscious hurt. Accept that this is your free choice, you are totally safe, and it is a completely natural process. Relax and take slow deep breaths as you feel emotion surfacing. Allow tears to come and waves of emotion to flow freely through your body. Do not force yourself or be judgmental of your ability to cry or not. Maybe you will shed a lot of tears or perhaps simply have a little weep, depending on what is right for you at this time. Trust in the Higher Self and know you are exactly where you are supposed to be during this learning experience. This is your healing process and all is well.

Take all the time you need and then, when you feel ready, return slowly to your normal state of consciousness. Thank your protectors for looking after you. You may choose to take a shower or bath if not already in one.

Open the window to let the energy out. Enjoy a long drink of water to help internal cleansing. Change the music to something a little livelier.

Now, stop to consider the experience. You will feel different from when you began. If anger arose accept it as part of the healing. Perhaps you may be sleepy, need air, feel lighter, more sensitive. Visualise yourself as radiating pure love and know this love protects you. Practise this Ritual whenever your need arises. Do not be surprised if the need lessens as emotional backlogs clear.

THE MOON EXERCISE

Although the Moon is astrologically associated with female energy this does not exclude males. Every human has influences of both the male and female and the protecting aspect of the Moon is relevant to both.

As a psychic since childhood I have been highly susceptible to attracting negative as well as positive energy. Instinct told me to use white Light from the Source for protection but, without practical instruction, it took a lot of practise to learn to visualise it. Before fully appreciating the value of spiritual protection I chose to explore the Darkness without realising the danger. I now know this was a necessary though unpleasant part of my personal spiritual development but it took its toll and, for a time, I suffered unhappiness, ill health, terror, confusion, and grief. I was able to heal myself once I knew the energy for protection and healing is the same.

Spiritual protection is most simply described as Light. Although it has nothing to do with light as we know it, attempting to describe this force would be like trying to draw a picture of the wind.

The protective spiritual Light that healers and other psychics use is accessible to everyone and it is strongly advisable not to try any esoteric experience without evoking it, otherwise one could well become embroiled with the powers of Negativity. Here are some techniques for using the Light to protect.

The Circle

Close your eyes and ask for protection from whatever form of Universal Goodness you follow. Imagine a spiral of white Light coming directly in from this Source and cocooning your body. Visualise the purity of moonlight as an example if necessary. Once this image is captured in your mind's eye it will be possible to create it instantly in times of physical threat.

By introducing the Light into such a situation you are positively illuminating the Darkness around you.

Protection of Home and Property

There are different methods of doing this. One is to visualise everything surrounded by the Light. I performed this ritual with my bender tent at Greenham Common some years ago. Astral Travel allowed me to rise from the physical body in order to view the exact pattern of Light surrounding it. The bender stayed safely in place for eight months while those around it were regularly removed by bailiffs. Occasionally I was woken from sleep by the image of a knife coming through the plastic. When the bender was finally destroyed, two months after I left, it was by vandals with knives.

When moving into a new home it is highly advisable to get rid of energy left behind by previous tenants. Visualise the Light flowing through rooms, cupboards and other storage areas, attic, garden, under the bed – everywhere within the perimeters of the place you call home.

Pure salt from the oceans is closely aligned to the Moon and is a symbol of cleansing. It also absorbs negativity. Place bowls of sea salt crystals in the four corners of your rooms and, surrounding yourself with Light, ask all negativity to depart. Leave the salt for seven days and do not store any refuse indoors. Dispose of the salt under running water.

Dried sage, a powerful herb for clearing negativity, may be lit and carried smouldering through the house where its smoke will permeate the atmosphere to cleanse and purify.

Protection against Fear

Fear may arise in a threatening situation as terror of the unknown or even fear of being alive. As enlightenment grows so does all fear dissolve but this may not be fast enough for some. It can quickly be eliminated by visualising the Light radiating outward from your Heart Chakra to surround you. The area of spiritual illumination can be as extensive as you need at the time although with practice it can be made large enough to embrace the whole world.

MERCURY

My dear friend, clear your mind of cant ...
You may talk in this manner; it is a mode of
talking in Society: but don't think foolishly.

Samuel Johnson 1709-1784

Colour: Yellow. **Symbols:** The Mind/Consciousness.
Energy: Yin and Yang. **Rules:** Gemini/Virgo.
Mode: Mutable. **House:** 3rd. **Time of Year:** May 22-
June 21/August 24 - September 22. **Elements:** Air/Earth.
Chakras: Throat (5th)/Brow (6th). **Cycle:** 88 days.
Stones: Sapphire, Alexandrite, Aquamarine, Sardonyx,
Agate. **Metals:** Nickel, Mercury, Magnesium.
Traditional Association: Thought.
Some Herbs and Flowers: Buttercup, Yarrow, Mugwort,
Caraway, Dill, Fenugreek, Marjoram, Lily of the Valley,
Savory, Petunia, Parsley. **Vegetables:** Carrots, Fennel,
Potato, Celeriac, Kohlrabi. **Fruit:** Grapefruit. **Bach Flower
Remedies:** Cherry plum, Cerato, White chestnut, Sweet
chestnut, Vervain, Beech.
Associated Words: Intellect, Logic, Consciousness,
Rational, Learning, Analysis, Practical values,
Communication, Judgement, Questions, Knowledge,
Exploration, Ideas, Travel, Building bridges, Healing,
Wholeness, Connection, Speaking, Writing, Humour,
Inventiveness.

Mercury, first of the inner planets to the sun, has a mere
88 day orbit and is the smallest in the solar system. It

represents the mind and all its workings. Fleeting thoughts, passing through the mind like quicksilver, are rarely credited with having any power in their own right and yet every stage of human evolution began with a single thought. As does any change.

Consider every great work of art and design creative colours and textures that surround us in beauty. Each is essentially a product of the human mind. So too is weaponry, war, greed, manipulation and destruction.

The miracle of modern communication, one of Mercury's associations, is another result of the human thought process. Satellites and cables that feed radio, television, telephone, fax, computer and internet, mean we can keep in closer touch with each other and are more aware of other nations. Accessible travel , another of Mercury's associations, allows for heightened experience and personal growth.

While all of this is directly related to Mercury it is necessary to examine the thought process on a personal level in order to fully benefit from its planetary influence. Our thoughts operate like radio waves and are guided by the subconscious mind. They can be positive or negative, flexible or rigid. It does not take a psychic to see how the power of thought can influence life for better or worse. Positive thinkers are more likely to succeed whereas pessimists are hampered by imaginary woes. Some people are so entrenched in negative thoughts that they implicitly believe a malevolent Universal plot is waiting 'out there' with the express intention of making life difficult. Why bother trying if there is no hope of achieving a goal or improving one's lot? Why indeed. And how is there such certainty these stumbling blocks exist? Through habitual negative thought patterns denying there is any other way.

The Chakras ruled by Mercury are the throat, indicating communication, and the brow, or Third Eye, for logic and psychic ability.

The way we think influences every aspect of life – particularily health which is highly susceptible to state of mind. Have you ever, for instance developed a headache when worried? If so, here is a straightforward demonstration of how mental tension physically lessens blood flow to the brain. Medical research, having recognised the correlation between mind and body is now investigating, through the sciences of physics and chemistry, how quantum healing works.

The following Bach Flower Remedies are particularily associated with Mercury although I believe the full range is ruled by this planet in that they all work through the mind and attitudes affecting the emotions. Cherry Plum is for fear of losing the mind; Cerato helps trust personal judgement; White Chestnut is for when the mind will not stop or rest; Red Chestnut eases mental torment; Vervain is taken for mental strain; Beech relaxes a critical mind.

It is all too easy to be led astray if we are rigid. Flexible thought reminds us that we don't necessarily know all the facts or understand the intention behind someone's apparently negative actions. We may then opt to withhold judgement until the full picture is revealed.

Mercury also reminds us we can heighten or lower personal vibrations according to our thinking. On occasions when I go to a club or a party my thoughts subtly become Ego-based. 'Do I look attractive?' 'Will I meet someone nice?' 'Have a good time?' Initially it is as if these thoughts are unique to me, which they are, on one level. Yet, on another level, I instinctively know they come from a 'curtain vibration frequency' that is part of the collective consciousness – a 'track' of similar thoughts left behind by others who entered the building before me.

Collective consciousness has produced positive results through group prayer and spiritual meditation for peace and other worthwhile goals. Used negatively it can create mayhem, as in mob hysteria, and has furthered evil such as that of Hitler's far-reaching power.

As Mercury moves around the Zodiac it presents many opportunities to become conscious of all aspects of life symbolised by the planets in this book. When it reaches the same position in the Zodiac Belt where it was at our birth we are granted a powerful opportunity to gain insight into the relationship we have with our thoughts and to greatly raise our consciousness.

Mercury represents the ability to see truth in its entirety. An example of what this total consciousness entails may be taken from the basic human instinct to protect and be protected. This is natural and healthy in moderation but overprotection can result in denial of truth. A cosseted offspring finds it difficult to cope with the harsh reality of independent life when he/she leaves home. In contrast, someone who grows up unprotected will have an equally difficult time. Both may decide that success and happiness are impossible to attain. A healthy balance of consciousness in parents and child helps prevent this attitude from developing.

Using affirmations for spiritual growth is a worthwhile

aspect of positive thinking and incorporates such aspects of Mercury as conscious thought, communication, learning, healing, wholeness, connection and exploring. Affirmations are a powerful method of using mind visualisation to dispel ingrained negative thoughts by replacing them with Light, Love, and a link to the Source of all Goodness. Through simple concentration we can introduce the possibilities of joy, freedom, improvement and goodness into our life. An addictive personality, for instance, can be set on the road to recovery through affirmations once a decision is made to end the abuse. Affirmations, when used as part of the collective consciousness, can even help rebalance this lovely planet on which we live. One of my favourites is, 'It's safe not to know.' Sometimes, when not feeling in control of a situation, my old fears resurface . By reminding myself that 'It's safe not to know,' I feel Creation supporting me and can relax again, trusting that the answers will be given at the right time.

When choosing or composing an affirmation for the first time try not to stray too far from your present situation or thoughts as this may create confusion between the conscious and subconscious mind. Perhaps you could start with something like, 'I love and am loved'. Use only positive words as these ingrain what you say in the subconscious mind. It helps to write it out in large clear letters and attach the page to a wall where you will see it often, therefore further compounding the thought in your beliefs.

Using affirmations negatively, for greedy or selfish purposes, only serves to further separate an individual from the Greater Good. Focusing the mind on unconditional love and better distribution of the world's wealth is an infinitely higher aspiration than to visualise a customised personal jumbo jet. Those who work towards fulfilling their Highest Potential will receive all the material support necessary.

Mercury also reminds us of the many facets of the mind. While concentrating on the positive it is also important not to deny, reject or bury negative aspects of the Self because this is part of the duality of human nature. Mercury's energy is both Yin and Yang, indicating balance. On this physical plane perfection can only be an aspiration, not a reality.

Travel, which Mercury rules, is one way to realise the flexible or limiting aspects of our beliefs. Through exposure to other cultures we sample different tastes, sounds, smells, and are confronted by erroneous assumptions we may have held. My consciousness was expanded through travel as I witnessed the level of suffering patiently endured by others. Their generosity and willingness to share what little they had was a marvel to behold.

Travel in any form is a liberating experience. If physical or astral travel is not possible we can still visit foreign places through the experience of others. Having 'wings on your heels' in the Mercurial sense means we can also traverse the Earth by skipping along the printed page – ruled by Mercury. Just as travel broadens the mind so too do good books and films by providing new insights and expanding our horizon.

Spending the major part of my life without books

meant I relied on experience and verbal communication for 'outside' information. Sometimes I found myself comfortably discussing topics that I had no logical reason to know anything about. Yet people listened. At first it was disturbing to find myself accurately answering questions about the lives of others when they asked but I eventually accepted being psychic. For a time I felt unique in spite of scepticism from many people but, as spiritual awareness grew, I realised this is a normal facet of human existence present in everybody. Some cultures naturally accept this ability. That such a gift is regarded as frightening, or has its existence denied, is an indication of how far humanity has strayed from Truth. It is only by re-connecting with natural intuition, and accepting guidance from our Higher Self, that we can make choices leading to a happier and more tranquil life. The Mercury Exercise later in this chapter is formulated to help create an awareness of your own psychic ability.

THE MERCURY RITUAL

This is intended to help liberate the mind from limited thinking. Prepare by using the guidelines from previous rituals. Choose candles and clothes in Mercury's warm yellow and smear any safe source of heat, such as radiator or lightbulb, with a little oil from the herbs or flowers aligned to the Planet.

Now, sit or lie down, close your eyes, breathe slowly and deeply, think about the environment you have created for this ritual and ask for spiritual protection. You are now going on a journey in your mind.

Think of yourself, at this moment, as an individual. Be

aware of your body. Consider how you exist on many different levels. You have a body and you are more than that. You have feelings and you are more than that. You have thoughts and you are more than that. You are Spirit and you are more than that.

Allow your mind to drift and memories to flow gently through you. Take your thoughts back to before you began this ritual, back through today, through yesterday, the day before, last week, last year. There is no need to try and remember every detail. Just allow key memories to comfortably come to mind.

Float back through the years, teens, childhood, even the moment of your birth. If possible keep going. Previous lives can be freely explored in the most enthralling history lesson ever. Accept images of obscure, famous or infamous historical events, be rich or poor, on land or sea, animal, vegetable or mineral. See volcanoes erupting, rocks being created, and crystals growing, With practise it may become possible for you to eventually go back into the Eternal Consciousness and relish the purity of the Source.

Now gently reverse the process and slowly move forward in your mind. Take all the time you need. Come through your present and future life span and out into space. Float effortlessly among the stars, asteroids, and planets, in the silent tranquillity of space. Go further into the Universe towards the Light and once again bask in the Source of all Goodness.

If at any time you feel you are getting too 'high' practise slow deep breathing for a minute or two. This simple step is a useful technique to ground yourself in this or any life situation.

When you feel ready, return slowly to the present moment through a reversal of the original steps. Come back to Earth, to your home, to your relaxed and comfortable body.

Keep your eyes closed as you become conscious of your surroundings. Consider for a few moments how it is consciousness that is the human essence rather than place, time, or the physical body. Thank your Guides for their protection and continue to sit or lie for as long as necessary before opening your eyes. You may feel a little tired after such a far-flung journey on ' Air Mercury'.

We learn, through this Ritual, that it is possible to change our relationship with Truth through conscious thought. It is our individual choice to view life from the confines of daily existence or from the spiritual knowledge that part of us has always existed and will continue to exist. There is no birth or death of the Eternal Spirit.

At another time try exploring 'inner space' by allowing your mind to move into your body, through the skin, into the bloodstream, through there into muscles, organs, sinews, nerves, tissues, cells, molecules, DNA, atoms, neutrons, and so on, into the centre of the core of your being. It is not necessary to name each part of your body as you visualise the journey. Here too the Creator of all Love is awaiting your arrival. The return journey is, as before, an unhurried reversal of the ritual. Have you noticed whichever route we take, internal or external, the destination is invariably the same? It just takes some longer to get there than others. Limited thinking? Never again.

THE MERCURY EXERCISE

This helps to connect with one's psychic ability and requires two people. As Mercury rules communication it is appropriate the experience is shared with someone who also wishes to explore this fascinating aspect of existence. By experimenting together you can support each other through change and growth. As humour is another aspect of Mercury's influence feel free to laugh like hyenas if the occasion arises.

If a suitable partner does not immediately come to mind ask for help from your Spiritual Guides/Guardian Angels who will then steer you towards meeting someone appropriate. Our needs are provided for in all sorts of inexplicable ways once we are truly open to receiving support from the Creator.

Psychic ability is like being a human radio receiver. This exercise helps to open the mind and enhances the ability to listen, not just to hear. It is inevitable that some mistakes will be made while venturing outside the boundary of everyday senses which is a natural part of every learning experience. Experimenting with your inbuilt 'aerial' and accepting 'static' makes it easier to tune into the correct frequency.

To begin, one partner becomes the psychic 'Explorer' while the other agrees to play a passive role. These roles may be reversed later. It is important both parties agree to protect the confidentiality of this occasion. When working with Mercury, communication needs to be kept open and clear in order to avoid misunderstandings.

Create a safe suitable atmosphere. Light yellow candles and hold a Mercury-associated stone to attract the planet's energy. Protect your environment with light (see the Moon Exercise) and both of you ask for spiritual protection to ensure you will only receive insights that will develop the Higher Self.

Now, sitting opposite each other, take several slow deep breaths to relax. Throughout the exercise you may have your eyes open or closed, either is fine.

The Explorer takes the 'driver's seat' and affirms that he/she is open to Guidance and declares an intention of tuning into personal psychic abilities. Then he/she lets go of preconceptions, intellectual understanding, and fear.

While this is happening the Partner concentrates on relaxing and mentally affirms trust in Guidance, the Explorer, and the situation.

Now it is time for the Explorer to allow further movement into the deeper recesses of his/her mind. Take plenty of time. Relax, this cannot be rushed.

It is important throughout this exercise that you do not push yourself beyond what feels comfortable. Remember to take long deep breaths if you need grounding at any stage.

Within this stillness and tranquility you will become aware of moving into a powerful state of heightened sensitivity. Move your attention slowly to your Partner. Different thoughts will come to mind. Speak them aloud and accept this as part of learning. They may be mundane, startlingly profound, or daft enough to provide a good fit of giggles for you both. Laughter might be the perfect release of tension. Sharing these thoughts with your Partner will further open your psychic channel. Let them go now and concentrate further. Speak slowly and clearly as other thoughts form while your Partner listens silently.

A pause will occur naturally. Use this to ask your Partner for feedback. Did anything you said seem relevant or useful to her/him? If so, it indicates the channel is opening. Discuss these insights and enjoy whatever humour they contain.

When you are both ready, within a reasonably short period of time, resume the exercise. At some stage your energy will begin to drop which is a natural indication to rest or stop. Follow the energy rhythm of your body and cease if the Ritual no longer feels comfortable. The overall result of this session may reveal a natural ability to tune into another person. If not, it simply means more practise is needed. In time it will be possible to channel for longer periods and you will have less need of a partner as your psychic ability grows stronger. The more we exercise any part of us, the stronger it – and we – become.

VENUS

How do I love thee? Let me count the ways.

Elizabeth Barrett Browning (1806 - 1861)

Colours: Pink, Green. **Symbol:** Unconditional Love. **Energy:** Yin. **Rules:** Taurus, Libra. **Mode:** Fixed and Cardinal. **Houses:** 2nd and 7th. **Time of Year:** April 19 - May 19/September 22 - October 21. **Elements:** Earth, Air. **Chakra:** Heart (4th) **Cycle:** 225 days, **Stones:** Emerald, Sapphire, Rose quartz, Lapis lazuli. **Metal:** Copper.

Traditional Association: The Lover. **Some Herbs and Flowers:** Daisy, Bluebell, Columbine, Hydrangea, Rose, Bergamot, Bleeding Heart, Elderflower, Foxglove, Lady's mantle, Mallow, Spearmint, Primrose, Self-Heal, Violets, Columbine, Hollyhock.

Vegetables/Pulses: Artichoke, Asparagus, Sorrel, Peas, Beans, Lentils. **Fruit:** Grapes, Pomegranate, Autumn Berries, Peach, Pear, Strawberries.

Bach Flower Remedies: Beech, Crab Apple, Schleranthus, Water Violet.

Associated Words: Love, Attraction, Beauty, Magnetism, Balance, Peace, Sensuality, Harmony, The Physical, Justice, Partnership, Truth, Aesthetics, Giving, Harmony, Co-operation.

Venus is that friendly twinkling light nearest where the Sun sets and rises. It represents love and the magnetic power of attraction while ruling the earthy Taurus and balanced Libra. Through this 'triangle' we can begin to see the influence it brings to our life. Couple this with the colours aligned to Venus – pink for spiritual love and green for personal love – and the picture becomes even clearer. Everything points to the beauty of true harmony.

The Bach Flower Remedies attuned to Venus help prepare the individual to give and receive love. Beech addresses unconditional acceptance for those who feel critical, cold, narrow-minded and judgmental; Crab Apple enhances healthy love of Self; Schleranthus creates balance through the heart; Water Violet dispels aloofness, arrogance and pride, enabling one to positively give and receive of the emotions.

At some point most people fall in love – and not always in adult life. Real and sincere love takes many forms. It may be toddler's adoration of mummy (or teddy bear), a child's love for a pet, teenage 'infatuation', fleeting adult romance, or deep abiding love that lasts a lifetime.

Whatever the duration, feelings are no less acute for the individual of any age. A child's pure love is given openly and freely – a precious gift, indeed. Young romance, often patronisingly referred to as 'puppy love', is no less real than that experienced by adults. Emotions are more intense when youthful vulnerability is coupled with developing hormones. Honest memory recalls that the time-span of the relationship bears no relation to the intensity of feelings involved – regardless of what parents may have claimed. ('You couldn't possibly be in love, you've only known him/her for a week!')

It is normal to have several romantic liaisons in adult life as few are lucky enough to find true love first time around. But at this stage of our evolutionary and social growth humanity has taken on a complex tapestry of beliefs that sometimes cloud and complicate expectations of ourself and our 'ideal' partner. We may be confounded with choice from a melting pot of previously inaccessible cultures – Aborigine to Amazon – and a host of genders.

Whether heterosexual, homosexual or bi-sexual, most people hope to eventually find a soul mate. This quest may entail a series of unintentional casual relationships as we seek the qualities with which Venus is associated – beauty, magnetism, sensuality, pleasure.

When it does not work out we part and try again – until finding a way through the emotional maze of choices and pressures seems almost impossible.

The most important thing to remember is that love will find us if we trust it to. This does not mean retiring from the social whirl but rather to change the reasons for going out. Give up looking over a shoulder or scanning every crowded room for 'the right one' unless you are intent on finding heartache, and, instead, allow love to come to you.

An individual's definition of true love may not always be correct. It can mean different things at various stages of life. When I was a teenager love struck like a lightning bolt, transforming my perfectly ordinary boyfriend into a god. Later on, marriage taught me that love is about giving as well as receiving and it required trust, loyalty, patience, and compromise without resentment. A blend of surrender and self control, receptivity and assertiveness, helped maintain the relationship. Still my marriage broke up without logical reason when I was 21. We had two great children and a nice home, but one day we just did not want to be together any longer. It seemed as if love had suddenly sprouted wings and flown out the window. We parted and remained friends which is, of course, another equally precious kind of love. Perhaps we were just too young to begin with.

Later I learned the difference between love and sexual attraction; that love can change from passionate to platonic; it can grow or evaporate; that love is not just something to get from a partner. What I sought from my lover was the bliss of feeling connected and letting go in order to surrender to something greater than the Self, but only when I got in touch with the Divine did I really began to understand.

I learned to use ritual in order to invoke the Goddess energy and, through it, developed an acute awareness of the pure love of the Divine flowing through my every cell.

It was amazing to discover this atmosphere is possible to create without a partner and to understand a true sense of Wholeness. I was better equipped to approach a partnership knowing what it means to give, rather than expecting my needs to be fulfilled by another.

Through the influence of Venus we learn that a relationship does not exist alone but rather is a third entity between two people and can only exist from what both parties put into it. Like a rose it needs care and nurturing. If we take without giving – pluck away the petals, cut the stems, forget to water it – the favourite flower of Venus will die.

Making love with Venus energy is a gentle, pleasurable union between consenting partners where there is a happy balance of sensuality, power, beauty, and responsibility. Lustful passion belongs in the realm of Mars.

The receptive Venus state is traditionally associated with women while men are more likely to display aggressively passionate Mars energy. This situation is now slowly changing as we move into the enlightened Age of Aquarius. Men and women are no longer satisfied to be incomplete, relying on partners for their own missing qualities. In this process of becoming whole, however, there can be a tendency to swing off balance. Women who are integrating with Mars energy can initially become worriers and unable to receive love from others. They have long craved, and are now claiming, all the Mars qualities that men are encouraged to possess from an early age – independence, freedom, power, success, and respect. Men, on the other hand, still look to women to provide the Venus energy and, without it, feel unloved or excluded. Male hurt often manifests in aggression, or exaggerated Mars energy, in an effort to compensate. A man who feels threatened in this way is more likely to 'turn the volume up' rather than allow himself to recognise, experience, and accept his vulnerability. Finding the courage to do so reinforces his capacity for sensitivity and love.

Many contemporary males are at a loss to know who they are and what is expected from them by women. The old macho stereotype is hard work, alien to many, and besides, it does not 'pull the birds' like it once did. Today's life, for a man, increasingly revolves around making money and accumulating materialistic status symbols – often at the loss of such basic human rights as happiness, and contentment.

He can re-identify with Venus energy by allowing more pleasure into his life and this will, in turn, connect him with his natural human instincts. Only through using these long-buried instincts can he come to understand who he is and know his place in the way of things. With this new awareness he begins to take better care of himself, becomes more attractive and learns that real men do cry when they discover the courage to let go instead of hiding pain behind a miserable barricade of 'manly control'. He will also be better able to express the receptive aspects of the Self.

Earthly life experience is similar to that of being in a school with a specifically formulated series of lessons, the first and most important of which is to love unconditionally. Venus is the key to this. Personal growth and development is seriously hindered by not allowing love in because of fear or hurt. Rising above such negativity helps us to understand that love is purely a choice of how to be rather than an expectation. It is a gift to be shared rather than hoarded. By connecting with the Source of All Love we allow it to flow freely through us, into the world and through the Earth.

Common love inhibitors are insecurity, need, blame, judgement, possessiveness, control, guilt, suspicion, or any human condition that is not based in trust, truth, and respect.

By nature we are imperfect beings and only compassionate acceptance of this will lead us closer to our potential for love and spiritual goodness. Minds and hearts are capable of almost limitless expansion.

In a healthy partnership true love encourages understanding and tolerance of our own, and our partner's, limitations. And, should the relationship end, it helps us to accept, forgive and let go with love. In this way we replace hurt and anger with peace and beauty.

Another aspect of Venus is the Taurean experience of everyday physical pleasure. Enjoyment of such sensual delights as visual art, music, dance, theatre, food, flowers, fragrances, and making love with a cherished partner are not to be denied. All these pleasures, in moderation, may be seen as a celebration of life. Too much fun results in over-stimulation of the senses, numbing them and ultimately depriving us of further enjoyment.

In combining the sensuous aspects of Taurus with the balancing influence of Libra, we can appreciate the inexhaustible supply of love in the Universe. Let it flow through you.

THE VENUS RITUAL

This is formulated for anyone who is feeling a lack of love. In extreme cases an individual may cause regrettable behaviour by attempting to meet these needs in an inappropriate way. While lack of love may be causing unhappiness it is important to realise that everything happens as it should, when it should. Friday is dedicated to Venus so this Ritual is ideally performed weekly, for a month, on this day.

Arrange to be warm, comfortable, and unhurried. The Venus Ritual is a natural process and may be adapted to suit whatever is right for you. A tendency to depend on someone else for emotional support indicates it is best to learn this process alone. If, on the other hand, you wish to share the experience with your partner and it becomes sexual, be mindful that Venus love, not Mars, is its essence.

Retaining this basic nature enables the individual, with practise, to summon Venus energy any time it is needed.

The reclining position, on a settee or in bed propped up with lots of pillows, is best. You may, if you wish, light rose-scented candles and wear or hold a sparkling Emerald, Sapphire, piece of Rose quartz, or deep blue Lapis lazuli.

Breathe deeply to relax. Take notice of your body. Everything is fine. Close your eyes and slowly inhale three deep breaths while focusing on your heart area. Imagine a soft pink light flowing through the chest and swirling around the heart as if washing away sadness or loneliness. Use the exhalation to let go of this.

If you need to cry at any stage do so gently without effort. This is another way of flushing away hurt that may be clouding your experience of love. By regularly repeating this ritual the need to cry will gradually disappear as pain is replaced with love.

Focus again on the beautiful swirling pink light as it sweeps away all unhappy and unwanted feelings towards yourself, somebody else, or even a situation that distresses you. Continue your visualisation for five minutes or so before allowing this loving illumination to permeate your whole body.

Venus energy may be visualised as a beautiful woman or man, to remember as a loving friend. Next time you need to connect with the power of love may be in a situation where it is not possible to do this ritual and this friend is hovering, just waiting to be summoned. For convenience I will refer to this Venus as 'she'.

In your mind's eye see her smiling in front of you,

dressed in your favourite shade of pink or green. The love in her heart flows directly into yours, and through it, to every part of your being. Allow it to permeate your every cell, lighting the darkness with cleansing warmth. Feel your heart open to receive an endless supply of love that has the power to change your very being. Your need to take is being transformed into an enthusiastic need to give.

Venus offers you a gift symbolising unconditional love and you affirm your worthiness to receive it. Take it joyfully from her outstretched hands and, with thanks, hold it close to your heart as you allow her image to fade slowly.

Return to your surroundings at a leisurely pace, bringing the gift of love with you. Let everyday sounds enter your consciousness, wriggle fingers and toes, move your head from side to side, open your eyes and sit up slowly.

A practical extension of this ritual is to make or buy something that symbolises the Venus gift of love. Perhaps a gemstone to be carried or worn, a book of love poetry, rose potpourri or perfume, pink mug or teapot, green/pink stationery, diary, address book or even a keyring with a dangling heart.

It is very likely that the attitude of family and friends will change towards you, in a positive way, as you work to create more love in your life. Be aware of a newly enhanced ability to attract others and understand this is not to be misused. Venus is not a heartbreaker.

THE VENUS EXERCISE

Many of us have developed unique and creative ways to limit the amount of love we are offered. Some blame others for not providing it while the rest blame themselves. Blame is merely a bad habit that serves no useful purpose and only brings pain without hope of resolution. Taking positive action through this exercise eliminates it by creating more love and beauty.

Write a list asking what you do to provide love and pleasure in your world. If nothing comes to mind try the following love-related questions: Do I limit enjoyable situations? When did I last give somebody a gift just for fun? Can I remember the last time I said 'I love you' to another person? How long is it since I provided a special treat for somebody (or myself) in the fridge, bath, or wardrobe department? Am I taking reasonable care of my health and appearance? If something unexpected happened tomorrow what friend would I tell? Do I create pleasant surroundings in which to live? Is my home/flat/bedsitter comfortable and welcoming?

Add whatever other questions come to mind. Then, when the list is finished, read it aloud and answer each question as you go. Being less than honest or finding excuses to justify uncomfortable answers only wastes time. The result may be surprising. Are you the sort of person that you would want for a best friend or partner?

From this moment on allow Venus love to live within you, to be part of all you do, flowing through you into every atom of the Universe.

MARS

We know our will is free, and there's an end on't.

Samuel Johnson 1709-1784

Colour: Red. **Symbol:** The Will. **Energy:** Yang.
Rules: Aries and co-rules Scorpio. **Mode:** Fixed and
Cardinal. **Houses:** 1st and 8th. **Time of Year:** March 20 -
April 18 / October 22 - November 20. **Elements:** Fire,
Water. **Chakras:** Base (1st) Sacral (2nd) Solar Plexus
(3rd). **Cycle:** 687 days. **Stones:** Diamond, Bloodstone,
Agate. **Metal:** Iron.
Traditional Association: War.
Some Herbs and Flowers: Basil, Chives, Crowsfoot,
Hawthorn, Honeysuckle, Hops, Lupin, Mustard, Nettle,
Tarragon, Woodruffe. **Vegetables:** Leeks, Onion, Radish.
Fruit: Rhubarb.
Bach Flower Remedies: Impatiens, Holly, Elm, Vervain,
Vine, Centaury.
Associated Words: Anger, Assertion, Aggression, Drive,
Power, Sexuality, Courage, Action, Energy, Regenerative,
Competition, Discovery, Fight, Taking, Impatience,
Violence.

Mars, eighth planet of the Zodiac, represents free will.
Although humans are linked to every other living
organism as an integral part of the Universe the soul or
spirit operates entirely on free will. The choices we make,
with this individual freedom, greatly affect our spiritual
development.

In an average situation a child is under the care and protection of parents or guardians who make decisions for it at a decreasing rate until it is old enough to take responsibility. The generally accepted 'Age of Reason' in Western society is believed to be reached when a child is seven years old. Other cultures vary. By this stage the youngster is expected to know right from wrong and, at eighteen or twenty-one years of age, is deemed adult enough to finally assume full responsibility for his or her life.

Although it may be necessary for society to generalise in this way it is, nevertheless, important to acknowledge that free will is present from birth. The sooner an individual learns to recognise the consequences of personal actions the better he or she is equipped for life.

Example is a child's first learning experience and the 'Do what I say, not what I do,' mode of behaviour in role models leads to confusion at an early age if adult actions are at odds with advice. Such bewildering messages create a distorted understanding of free will in the child which in turn hampers growth in its spiritual awareness. The result can unhappily manifest as impatience, disrespect, fear, anger, aggression or violence.

Experience of growing entails experimenting with cause and effect. Old heads do not belong on young shoulders and sensible advice from parents is ignored as a child explores his or her environment with free will. Junior learns, among other things, that fire burns, poisons makes you sick, and there is less tolerance in the outside world than at home. Through their own free will parents or carers can let go of control in order to allow the child to learn from his or her mistakes without blame.

This same free will, the soul's glorious expression of individuality, also creates barriers and stumbling blocks if not used for the Greater Good. Every soul on earth is completely free to behave in any manner it chooses. Some people opt simply for an offensive personality, some go on to create murder, horror, and devastation, while others lead a life of love and respect for all things. Only an awareness of, and harmony with, the Divine separates the actions of one from the other. Every life situation presents a selection of options and personal choices. Free will allows us to move towards or away from the Light through its use or misuse.

When misfortune falls it may have been brought about through one or more acts of our own free will or is the result of karma built up in one or several previous incarnations. It may be interpreted as the 'Will of God'. Acceptance of this 'Will' does not mean relinquishing personal power, or free will, as demanded by some cults, sects, or sections of established religion. No person, group, or authority, has the right to interfere with the free will of the individual for, by doing so, the spiritual path of this soul is being manipulated. Nor is the 'Will of God' to be used as a means to avoid or relinquish responsibility for our life and actions. Free will of the individual means weighing up choices, making decisions, and responsibly accepting the consequences without blaming anyone or anything else. Negative situations arising from any decision is a lesson through which it is possible to gain greater spiritual awareness.

Reaction is also an expression of free will and

depending on whether it is negative or positive we are given the opportunity to further enhance or hinder spiritual development.

The everlasting diamond, with its powerful spiritual energy, is the stone most closely aligned to Mars. It is no accident this sparkling jewel traditionally symbolises a loving relationship. Wearing one or more diamonds enables us to be more vital, sensitive, and loving, by combining the Mars and Venus energy. It also helps enhance creativity in lovemaking.

Bach Flower Remedies aligned to Mars encourage positive aspects of the planetary energy. Impatiens brings out patience and gentleness; Holly enhances the capacity for unconditional love; Elm strengthens the ability to accept responsibility; Vervain works on self-discipline and restraint; Vine fortifies wisdom in leadership; Centaury addresses determination and helps improve the will.

Opinions vary on what Chakras are related to Mars. While some say the planet is affiliated with the whole physical body, through the energy and drive that keeps it alive, I see a more specific connection with the lower three Chakras.

The solar plexus, (3rd), represents assertive will for actions based on the self-focused ego, while the coccyx (2nd) energises the reproductive system and stimulates the desire to reproduce and protect the young. The Base or Root Chakra (1st) motivates the will to survive on Earth.

Anger and aggression are other aspects of Mars. It is no accident that the ancient God of War and this planet share the same name. In the negative Mars is associated with hot, violent, male energy.

Understanding this enables us to more clearly express feelings without interfering in the free will of another. Anger is a natural human emotion and it is healthy to feel like this sometimes. In situations of conflict we can dare to speak our truth while being prepared to hear the truth of the other party. Only in personalising anger and directing it at another – by lashing out verbally or physically – does the trouble begin. The recipient of this venom then feels attacked and usually reacts by striking out in defence.

Through openly feeling anger while resisting the temptation to direct it at someone else, we are helping to break a cycle of violence that pollutes our world. This does not mean storing it until it explodes in a seething rage, when our anger may become harmful, but instead consciously sending it back into the Universe.

As a child, wanting everyone to like me, I began to suppress anger even though, by nature, I have a strong Mars energy. Later on it came as a shock when I was told people were scared of me. What I did not know then is that consciously-suppressed true nature still comes through in the subconscious. I was virtually seeping anger. With this knowledge I began to use healthy ways, such as swimming and aerobics, to burn off destructive Mars energy while focusing, single-mindedly, on Higher Awareness. Hakomi therapy enabled me to shed much of the old buried resentment and frustration. Now I am able to achieve more than I ever imagined.

Another Mars-associated word is 'Power'. Many individuals are unaware of their personal power and only see this word in relation to figures of authority. Rulers, politicians, law enforcers, health professionals, corporate executives, employers and management, the wealthy, landlords, instructors, enablers, guardians and parents, are just some of those regarded as being powerful. But the only power anyone can acquire is what we, as separate beings, allow them to take.

Although many powerful people have helped create goodness and beauty, not everyone understands how to use this strength responsibly. In daily life we see abuse of power manifested as lack of compassion or disrespect. It may be in the exploitation of a single worker or violent manipulation of the masses through warring power struggles. As a result many individuals, particularily women, suppress personal power through fear of abusing it themselves or becoming like those who do.

Supposing you are in a situation of continual conflict. Let's say, for instance this is happening in the workplace. By allowing oneself, as 'victim', to go overboard to please the 'aggressor' you are giving your power away and eventually one of you will probably be forced to leave. This may temporarily ease things but nothing has been done to resolve the situation. It is only a matter of time before you attract some other 'aggressor'. That is, unless you reclaim your power, challenge the 'aggressor', and put a stop to the conflict.

My personal way of dealing with this is to remember that I have disowned parts of the Self in the past, as we all do, and when the time is right to reclaim them I meet people who embody those qualities I now need to acknowledge and integrate. With this in mind we can learn to see this other person as an aspect of ourself and

70

accept that our heart is the centre of balance.

Reminding yourself of unconditional love, calling on spirit Guides or Angels, expressing grievances, and asking them for help to connect with the Source, will create the means to resolve an unpleasant situation.

Power is a natural energy and when used correctly can achieve wonderful things. Mars rules Aries, first sign of the Zodiac, the aspect of creativity. By aligning personal power to the Highest form of Creation we can all learn to heal, forgive, survive, study, teach, nurture children, grow food, and create positive energy to achieve the future we deserve.

Mars is also strongly linked with sexual energy as in intense passion. Concentrating on the Mars drive, while excluding loving Venus, generally results in taking selfishly and forgetting the heart. This behaviour indicates disrespectful , irresponsible, and potentially harmful, lust.

There is nothing wrong with healthy passion when it is connected to goodness and spirituality but without this focus it may become abusive in the emotional or physical sense. When the influence of Mars creates high sexual passion it is important to retain respect for yourself, your partner, the situation, and to remember love. Allow Mars and Venus to come together in their own passionate embrace.

THE MARS RITUAL

Through this Ritual we can liberate personal Mars energy and further activate the free will to instigate healing of ourself and planet Earth. Creative self-expression, with dynamic energy, has an enormous effect on us and our environment. I have practised the following for many years and credit it with keeping my power open and flowing. It has three stages.

The hardest part is finding somewhere suitable to perform it, especially if living in a built-up area. I save it for walks in the countryside, by the sea, or among ancient monuments.

It entails issuing noise although, when done correctly, this will not frighten passers-by. The sound is more like a horn blowing than fearful shrieking.

Stage One

Find a place, indoors or out, where you can be alone or solely among chosen companions who wish to join in. Wearing red clothes will help keep you concentrated on the Mars energy. Stand loosely with body upright, knees slightly bent and feet at shoulder width – or slightly further – apart. Take a few deep breaths with each one getting slower. Now, fill your lungs to capacity and exhale slowly while confidently allowing a sound '... A-a-a-a-ahhhhh ... ' to escape at whatever volume feels comfortable. Do not force yourself or allow fear to silence you. Exhale fully, pulling in the stomach to expel all air, and resume your normal rhythm of breathing for the next few breaths. Repeat twice more and try to make a louder noise each time. Relax.

Stage Two

When you have done this ritual often enough for it to have become comfortably familiar try adding another dimension. Just before exhalation think of any anger you might be holding and imagine your outgoing voice can be heard as far as your eye can see.

For the second breath think of someone you know who is angry and visualise the sound sweeping throughout the entire country. Finally, on the third breath, think of all the people around the world who cannot cry out for any reason. This time visualise your voice soaring far out into the Universe and let this healing sound carry the anger far far away.

Stage Three

Protect yourself spiritually as described in the Moon Ritual. Repeat the exercise but this time slowly raise your arms above your head as the noise comes out. Simultaneously visualise a strong white light representing your power, clear and sparkling like a diamond, coming from your heart through the hands and out into the Universe.

Perceive your voice as a loving powerful force pouring out to empower all who hear it. Imagine that this sound can awaken other souls and help their Will to become aligned with the purest Source of Love as yours is now becoming.

I like to finish this Ritual by sitting or lying on the grass for a little while, allowing my inner space to fill with the new peace, thinking about the positive force of change and the silent cry of freedom resounding in hearts of those around the world who seek liberation from oppression and suffering.

Tuesday is associated with Mars and, while not essential, it may help to practise the ritual on that day at sunrise or sunset.

THE MARS EXERCISE

Mars energy is spontaneous and directs us to go after what we want from life. That sounds positive until we stop to consider – is what we want the best thing for us and for others? 'Be careful what you wish for – it might come true.' While asserting free will in chasing a goal it is vital we are prepared to accept that a Higher Power always knows better and will only provide what is for our greater good although we may not be able to see this at the time.

In everyday life we may allow lack of assertion to hinder us from achieving goals. Being timid or fearful is a hindrance to progress that may be eliminated through examining the belief system by which we have operated up to now. Take pen and paper and write down the answers to the following questions: What makes me feel strong and powerful? What makes me feel the opposite? What would I secretly like to achieve that I feel is beyond me? What is preventing this? Do I fear success? Do I fear failure? Do I fear the change to my life that either would bring?

Consider the result and honestly ask yourself if your fears are realistic or simply an excuse to avoid action. We may prefer not to follow a dream in case the reality turns out differently to what we expected.

Is it possible to end up losing a perfectly good dream without gaining anything? Oh, horrors! What on earth gave you the crazy idea there can only ever be one dream in your heart?

Remember you are never alone in anything you do. The Source of Universal Goodness and your personal Guides are forever on hand to offer help and support. Ask for it.

JUPITER

When we are grown and take our place
As men and women of our race.

Rudyard Kipling (1865-1936)

Colour: Purple. **Symbol:** Growth and Expansion.
Energy: Yang. **Rules:** Sagittarius. **Mode:** Mutable.
House: 9th. **Time of Year:** November 21 - December 20.
Element: Fire. **Chakras:** Brow (6th) and Crown (7th).
Cycle: 12 years. **Stones:** Amethyst, Turquoise, Topaz,
Malachite. **Metal:** Tin.
Traditional association: King or Emperor.
Some Herbs and Flowers: Aniseed, Carnation, Thyme,
Clover, Sage, Borage, Hyssop, Marigold, Dandelion,
Chervil, Meadowsweet. **Vegetables:**Asparagus, Celery.
Fruit: Grapefruit, Currants, Sultanas.
Bach Flower Remedies: Rock Water, Hornbeam.
Associated Words: Magnify, Force, Exaggerate, Enthuse,
Broad, Luck, Philosophy, Travel, Explore, Trust, Faith,
Vision, Optimism, Abundant, Excess, Belief, Education,
Grace.

Jupiter, with its four moons, is the largest planet to
orbit the Sun. Its energy is firmly directed towards growth
and expansion.

Human growth is physically underway from the
moment of conception but not until birth does the infant
also begin to expand mentally, emotionally, and
spiritually. Parents nurture a child with love, care, food,

warmth and gentleness and help its senses to develop and expand through a variety of tastes and touches. They surround it with colour and agreeable sounds, from cooing to lullabies, until it believes its little Self to be the Most Important Being in the World. Then, at some point, this precious wee thing reaches out to find the boundaries of its cosy world and, in doing so, invariably incurs the displeasure of one or both parents, usually for its own safety. And so this new member of society learns, grows, and really begins to expand its awareness. This situation is, of course, the ideal.

Another baby does not have such an easy beginning. It may be unwanted, unloved, underprivileged, orphaned. This child also learns from its environment and in doing so grows and expands alone, in its own way, for better or worse. Extensive research tells us that an unloved child does not grow or develop at the same rate as its more privileged counterpart. Crowded orphanages in Eastern Europe and elsewhere bear heartbreaking examples of what occurs when carers are too overworked and have not enough time to spend with each child.

While a soul chooses, before birth, the parents and environment most suitable to expand its spiritual development this cannot be used as an excuse to ignore the desperate plight of these children. It is quite possible they may have chosen to incarnate in this situation with the express intention of raising the level of our compassion.

If only we could change the world. But we cannot ... or can we? The romantic notion of riding out like a knight in shining armour to put everything right belongs firmly wedged between the pages of a fairytale, but we can, as individuals, instigate positive change that will eventually embrace the Earth.

Spiritual awareness, like charity, begins at home. It begins in the heart of each indvidual. Through the energy of Jupiter we learn to refine personal growth and, in this way, contribute to the Greater Good.

It is impossible to consciously remember what it felt like the first time we pinched the cat, sucked a piece of coal, or pulled the ears off teddy, but we happily accept those segments of our development can be taken for granted. However, opportunities for growth and expansion are present for as long as we exist.

Adults continue to develop through relationships with other people, events or experiences. Depending on how we choose to react to these we either grow and expand or shut down and shrivel. When Jupiter is affecting a particular area of life it intensifies that experience so that we are provided with the opportunity to learn, evolve, and move on to the next phase. But as the planet's energy is unable to discriminate it also enables negativity to grow and expand unless the free will is focused on Goodness. Just as such spiritually aware traits like tolerance, kindness, and love are enhanced by Jupiter's influence, so too, for instance, is jealousy, envy, greed, or violence. This energy expands anything with which it comes into contact.

Imagine a large glass ball filled with Juniper energy. Pour in a trickle of water and it becomes an ocean. Lower in a man who eats a lot of fattening food and see him getting fatter. Drop in an angry woman and watch her anger intensify. Slip in a loving, peaceful person and notice love and peace grow and flourish. In this ball a good thought becomes a good reality and an evil thought becomes an evil reality.

Supposing somebody decided, in a previous life, that love was not a possibility for him or her and carried that unresolved thought pattern into this incarnation. Jupiter will support the belief this time around and every unloving thought and action will grow until life unhappily becomes all this person believes it to be. So is the opposite true. Working through the Light with Jupiter energy expands positive experiences to create joy and spread happiness. Negative behaviour, generally based in fear, is inclined to take the 'easy way out' and only succeeds in expanding the Darkness.

Because Jupiter has no boundaries the possibilities for evolution are limitless and, for this reason, it is crucial we choose to align with the Divine. Our thoughts create only what we believe and nothing except limited thinking creates those limits.

Thought forms, aligned with free will, determine our direction in life. We come from the Source of All Life and that is where we shall return.

The Bach Flower Remedies formulated to enhance the positive aspects of Jupiter influences are: Rock water to loosen tight reins such as rigidity, denial, perfectionism; Hornbeam to assist in carrying projects through to completion and release limitations.

Jupiter also urges us to expand our understanding of the Greater Plan. That nothing happens by 'accident' and everything is ordained that we may have the choice of progressing towards the Light. It encourages us to have faith, trust and confidence in the Self and life in general.

The Chakras associated with Jupiter are the brow, site of the Third Eye, and the crown which, like Jupiter and the colour purple, is associated with royalty and inspirational leadership. The Third Eye is the area of psychic 'sight' associated with mediumship and sensitivity. Allowing the Third Eye to develop means we are better able to tune in to a course of action that will reveal personal potential and, by integrating it into society, will contribute positively to the whole. Through Jupiter's power of expansion a loving heart will find the best way to move forward.

THE JUPITER RITUAL

The key to growth, expansion, and development, lies in the willingness to embrace change. And the key to change is being able to confidently acknowledge the 'Now' – this very moment. It is not possible to change the past but we can influence the future through our actions in the present. Only by being consciously present in each life experience can we give it our full attention and this is where Jupiter energy can be of enormous help.

Have you ever, for instance, spent time at work unable to concentrate on the job in hand because you were worrying about some problem at home? Then, back at home again, you find yourself worrying about being unable to concentrate at work? This is a classic example of not being in the Now.

In this situation it becomes impossible to rest properly because of worry about what is likely to happen tomorrow or next week. By the time tomorrow comes we feel unable to cope because of not being able to relax and therefore to regenerate. Is it any wonder things get on top of us?

Focusing on what is directly ahead, instead of scanning all the options, is the route to Jupiter-influenced growth and expansion. By being completely present at each experience we can give it full attention and deal with the project or situation to the best of our ability. To be successful at work we need to give it our full concentration. Then, at home, we are better able to fully experience the joy of spending time with a loving family as we talk, work, laugh and live together in a relaxed way.

The Jupiter Ritual is designed to help us focus on the Now and may be done at any time although Thursday is the weekday connected with this planet.

You will need dried sage or cedar for burning, a ceramic, glass, or pottery bowl, preferably in Jupiter's purple or yellow, three of the Jupiter gemstones or tokens in their colours.

Begin by spiritually cleansing and protecting yourself and the immediate environment. Soak your equipment for no less than 20 minutes in a solution of sea salt crystals dissolved in boiling water. Then ask the Highest Power to increase naturally, harmoniously and easily, for the good of all, that which is placed in the bowl. Accept that Creation knows what is best and will provide that for you.

Take each gemstone or token, one at a time, in the palm of your hand, close your eyes and focus on your intention for a minute or two until your thoughts are absolutely clear. Place gently into the bowl and leave them there for seven days. This ritual is particularily potent if done during Jupiter's own season, November 21-December 20.

This time of year, incorporating the Winter Solstice, is highly appropriate for visualising positive aspects you wish for in the year ahead.

During the seven days you may sit in front of the bowl whenever you wish to meditate on abundance and trust. When the time is up remove the tokens while thanking Creation for all the goodness, help, and abundance you have received in your life.

Never overwork this Ritual by using too often or for greedy or selfish purposes. Remember it is based on Expansion and will also intensify these negative traits.

As it becomes more familiar with practise you may wish to include other objects in the bowl. These can take the form of written affirmations, photographs, representational pictures, money or gifts – anything that symbolises a positive and unselfish wish.

THE JUPITER EXERCISE

When Jupiter is activated it feels as if you are astride a wild stallion who is galloping towards the future. Sometimes, when we are unsure of the best course of action to take, we may feel like leaping on this animal as a diversion and galloping about just for the sheer hell of it. Having fun in this way is fine – only it may not always be possible to get the stallion to take you home safely when you have had enough. Remember this horse is wild and may very well carry you off-course if your intentions are unclear.

In this event you might as well resign yourself to accepting, even enjoying, the learning process that brings you back to base on foot, unaided by the powerful planetary force of Jupiter. While you are trudging along consider the thought process that brought you into this situation, to this very spot, at this exact moment in time.

To avoid 'wild horse chases' in life we need to examine our intentions and choose a direct course of positive and conscious action that will take us as far as we ultimately wish to go, trusting in a Higher Power for guidance. Choosing a direction is more satisfying than opting for short term fear-based 'jaunts' which take a lot of unravelling later as we try to extricate ourselves from unsatisfactory situations.

Think of each course of positive action as a strong faithful stallion. You have an entire stable of them at your disposal and any one can help you to win the race. When the time is right for each horse to run, trust it to find you. By mounting it with clear intentions you may head straight for the winning post

Now, for this exercise ask yourself, if your life were to end an hour from now, would you have any regrets? Remorse? If so, can the situation be rectified now? Think of all the people who reach the end of this incarnation berating themselves for what they did or did not do. Many lives are spent in resentment, blame, stress, apathy, or other loveless conditions. What a sad waste. How much more satisfying it would be to move on knowing you have loved, laughed, learned, forgiven your enemies, forgotten your woes and respected yourself and your environment.

Take a pad and draw three columns. In the first make a list of what you consider to be 'unfinished business' with other people that it is in your power to rectify. This may be as simple as replying to a letter or as complex as laying a family feud to rest. In the second column list your ambitions – to visit the zoo, gain a diploma in Aeronautical Design, change your hair colour, climb a pyramid or plot the definitive map of Ancient Celtic Rock Pools. The third column is to list ways you can work towards reaching the degree of spirituality you wish to attain in this life.

It might show relevant book titles, addresses of awareness groups you intend to join, shopping lists (candles, stones, incense), sites to visit, affirmations, meditations, guidelines to bring more spirituality into your everyday life. This could even turn out to be the longest list.

Any item on the page can be adjusted or developed as time passes and new options come and go. But now you have the outline for a Life Plan that will help you to be more focused and to make informed choices. Be mindful that fresh opportunities are not necessarily an end in themselves but rather the means by which to learn how to reach your goal. Your stallion might be still in training. It will not be ready to run the race until it reaches peak fitness.

When you are finished pin the page on the wall and begin to work through the columns. Even with Jupiter's help it may take a lifetime to complete but the only time to begin is NOW.

SATURN

Poems are made by fools like me,
But only God can make a tree.

Alfred Joyce Kilmer (1886-1918)

Colours: Brown, Terracotta, Red/Brown. **Symbol:** Form and Structure. **Energy:** Yin. **Rules:** Capricorn.
Mode: Cardinal. **House:** 10th. **Time of Year:** December 21 - January 19. **Element:** Earth. **Chakra:** Root (1st). Cycle: 29.5 years. **Stones:** Quartz Crystal, Garnet, Onyx, Jet, Tiger's Eye. **Metals:** Zinc, Lead.
Traditional Association: The Truth-teller.
Some Herbs and Flowers: Myrrh (unless pregnant), Safflower, Pansy, Hellebore, Aconite, Mullein, Patchouli, Rosewood, Comfrey, Vetivert. **Vegetables:** All root vegetables. **Bach Flower Remedies:** Oak, Olive, Gentian, Gorse, Chestnut Bud, Larch, Willow.
Associated Words: Structure, Realism, Limit, Practical, Foundation, Mature, Respect, Work, Reward, Authority, Discipline, Clarity, Focus, Success, Crystallise, Enforce, Rigid, Fear, Guilt, Defensive.

Saturn, 'planet of the rings', takes twenty-nine and a half years to orbit the Sun and is the second largest planet in our solar system.

The symbol of Form and Structure indicates its influence on all aspects of physical life. Even the planet on which we live experiences this on all levels, from rocks to animated life form, in accordance with the laws of nature.

Just as the body has structure so too does life, as illustrated by the home, family, job, workplace, society, culture, government and environment. This operates positively through caring responsibility and discipline, with respectful authority, effort, organisation, patience, wisdom and reliability.

The negative side of this energy limits progress through fear, rigidity, guilt, defensiveness, lack of faith and too much self-reliance.

There are limits to any form and unfortunately, the negative aspects of Saturn's energy, the limitations, are more widely known than are its positive attributes. What really matters is how we approach, recognise and deal with these.

Take a work situation for instance. Everyone on earth has talents in some area of life but if we work at something where these talents are not employed we will almost certainly become discontented, even disillusioned, and unable to give the job our best effort. This sets up a chain reaction where the employer is unhappy, perhaps mistakenly believing we are devoid of talent, ambivalent about the job, lacking in motivation, and ultimately not worth the wages or salary. Boss berates employee who becomes even more incompetent. The usual conclusion is resignation or dismissal and sometimes the only difference between the two is split-second timing. Now the relieved boss is free to find somebody else while the newly liberated worker looks for another job better suited to his or her individual talents.

Degree, diploma or other certificate, achieved under pressure from an overcrowded education system, is no guarantee that a person is suitable for a particular job or profession. Surprisingly often a scan of mature workers in any workplace reveals few are still operating, from choice, in the work for which they were originally trained. In the changing structure of the contemporary workplace the rigid/secure 'job for life' belief no longer exists. Everything is changing. Only professional practitioners in such areas as medicine, law, and other traditional services, retain a degree of constancy in employment but even here the form and structure of the job is also changing.

Today it is barely surprising to see traditional businesses close down or merge, to find ourselves or our associates made redundant, or be offered the choice of re-training.

Rather than casting a slight on the worker's previous performance, re-training may be viewed as a wonderful opportunity to learn new skills better suited to individual talents or the chance to try something completely different which may have been a secret dream. If regarded as a valuable 'second chance', rather than relegation to the 'scrap heap', this can provide more enjoyment of life. Optimism says, 'Here is the opportunity to have a go without pressure.' Pessimism mutters, 'What's the point in learning anything else? I was okay at/enjoyed so-and-so and they didn't want me.' These are changes in form and structure in action – embrace them.

The nature of Saturn's energy is that if it gets too tight it can eventually manifest in spinal stiffness, heart problems or depression. If life structure is flexible, not rigid but rooted like a tree, we can bend with the winds of change and adjust to new ways without damage.

Swapping rigid thinking for a more open attitude allows us to become whatever we like, within sensible reason. The chances of a seventy-year-old bronchitic joining the Bolshoi Ballet are pretty unlikely but who has decreed that a book-keeper cannot become a graphic designer? That a truck driver cannot become a teacher? What is to prevent a printer from becoming an alternative healer? Nothing – except the necessary talent and the courage to instigate a shift in the form and structure of life.

Through realising we have been here before and may return many more times we begin to understand the importance of creating a lasting life structure based on the Highest Order. Some portions of life will be grounded in Truth while others are incomplete and still forming. Flexibility allows all to evolve into the Whole.

Learning to be patient and to trust means we do not have to take, manipulate or steal on any level of existence. A structure based on greed unbalances the spiritual condition of the soul or souls involved and, at some point, has to be re-balanced.

This is particularily apparent in the ecological vandalism taking place somewhere in the world right now in the name of big business. Reasonable profit is the rightful reward of all business and a vital part of its form and structure when practised with respect for human and other resources. Once profit evolves into greed everything that is practical, functional, and dignified, begins to evaporate to the eventual detriment of all concerned.

Within society we see everyday changes as structures that are not positively serving us crumble to dust. Changes were slower and more subtle in the past but with the advent of the New Age humankind is becoming more aware of the Greater Goodness that is at the core of life. Aspects of this may have gone temporarily overboard through sole reliance on individual resources and the need for social approval, as in extreme political correctness. But every pendulum needs to swing to extremes before settling and the pendulum of change is no exception. As we develop awareness of our spirituality, so too will love, respect, and individual happiness, increase.

Quartz crystal, aligned to Saturn, symbolises this aspect of form and structure. By allowing light to enter and shine through the crystal it radiates outwards, showering everything before it in a natural spectrum of clear intense colour. Block the light and the crystal becomes dull and brittle. Rigid adherence to old beliefs crystallises the individual until he or she become so brittle as to shatter at the slightest change. Blocked energy in the body also turns to physical crystals which are very difficult to break down.

The Bach Flower Remedies associated with Saturn's influence are: Gentian to overcome conflict and resolve difficulties; Gorse to re-establish hope and retrieve personal power for survival; Olive restores the survival instinct and personal strength; Chestnut Bud corrects past errors, helps manifest anything on the physical plane and redirects efforts to reach fulfillment; Oak increases courage and reliability and helps one to become strongly rooted in life's purpose in a relaxed way; Willow creates structure in life and helps one take responsibility for oneself; Larch improves self-esteem, increases confidence and practicality.

Saturn's energy encourages us to make the best of what is directly in front. This means self, personal health and grooming, caring for the home, partner, family, job or daily chores. Doing this allows the Higher Powers to help us reach our greatest potential, if we do it with Guidance.

Saturn and Mars share the Base or Root Chakra. In this instance, it provides a healthy connection with the earth. Through 'rooting' in the mother planet, like a tree, we are ensured of continual contact with nature and basic earthly needs.

THE SATURN RITUAL

The object of this Ritual is to become more harmonious with life. Through exploring and aligning with the nature of Creation we can participate in the organic process of creating personal life form and structure. Doing this in an appropriate way guides us towards realising our Highest Potential.

Think about a tree – the perfect example of nature's form and structure. It begins as a tiny seed and grows, slowly and steadily, into a huge oxygen-generating, shade, shelter, and, sometimes, food-providing, beauty. The root system reaching deeply into Mother Earth is almost as big as its branches and its tip is forever stretching towards the heavens.

This Ritual involves choosing one of the trees on which Saturn smiles, oak, yew, elm, poplar, willow, larch or chestnut, and the most effective day of the week is, naturally, Saturday. Wear earthy browns, red/brown and/or green, into a wooded area, and walk about for a while until instinct draws you to a particular tree. If you already have a favourite in any area, use it.

While facing the tree take your shoes off and sit on the ground next to it, spine straight, with the soles of your feet placed directly on the earth and consciously seek protection from your Guides.

Look kindly at 'your' tree, and notice how the trunk is solid and supportive. See the complex network of branches, leaves, fruit or flowers, how they are intertwined, connected to, dependent upon, the stable trunk. Consider how all of these have an annual life cycle of birth, growth, maturity and death, repeated a hundred times or more. How it stands there in all weathers giving more than it takes by helping to clean our air while offering food and shelter to human, animal, bird and insect through a precious and unique eco-system.

Bring your thoughts to the roots of this mighty plant. Visualise massive unseen 'toes' reaching down through the soil into the Earth to get nourishment while supporting the entire formidable structure.

Tune into the subtle energy of the tree. Sense the peace and healing coming from it and understand, as an organic life form, it also has a spiritual dimension. Take time to enjoy the relationship you share.

Now take some slow deep breaths and imagine your body as the trunk of a tree. It is strong, grounded, healthy and attuned to nature. Feel the solidity and life energy as you bring your attention down from the central trunk, along your vertebrae, to the base of your spine where the tail once grew. Visualise this tail and allow it to continue down into the earth as it roots you and strengthens your connection with the planet.

Slowly bring your attention to your feet. Enjoy wriggling those toes in the soil. Imagine roots growing from your feet into the ground, enhancing and strengthening your connection with the Earth. Close your eyes and consider the sublime spiritual nourishment provided by this act.

When you feel ready move back up your 'trunk' and consider how you are feeling. There is every possibility you will acknowledge the joy of being truly 'grounded' – a sense of spiritual and physical tranquility that everyone has a right to experience on a regular basis.

At this stage it is appropriate to take your thoughts to the outside world and consider the many branches of your life. You are in the centre, as the trunk, and those extending branches carry the leaves, fruits, and flowers that represent your beliefs, actions, and relationships. Whether they flourish or wither is your choice.

Draw the Ritual to an end, slowly and gently, by returning to your original state of consciousness and allowing a feeling of wholeness to permeate your body. Thank your Guides and the tree for being there and providing the experience. Wrapping your arms around the warm dry trunk with love is a perfect way to close. As you walk, skip, or dance away from that stationary tree remind yourself of how free you are to create your own structure.

THE SATURN EXERCISE

This is an on-going Exercise, extended over a period of time and may be regarded as a continuing meditation. Take a large sheet of firm card and draw a simple picture of a tree. The bigger the better, with a broad trunk, strong root system and lots of branches without leaves. This is not a test of artistic ability so please do not concern yourself with drawing skill or lack of it.

See each major branch as representing the many aspects of your life. Family, friends, job, hobbies, sports, home, pets, possessions. From the main branches add the smaller 'personal' boughs which represent your beliefs, aspirations, ambitions, happy memories, milestones, creative endeavours, lucky numbers, significant words or phrases, favourite places, and symbols of anything that inspires you.

Over a period of time fill all of these with a collage of 'leaves', representing the many wonderful aspects of your life. Make them from leaf-shaped pieces of coloured paper on which you have written words, dates or names, magazine cuttings, old greeting cards, sections of photographs.

Go on to include pressed flowers from a special place, tiny shells from your favourite beach, modelling clay symbols, small feathers, bits of jewellery, or anything else suitably representational.

Do not be surprised if the original tree drawing ends up being completely obscured by the abundance of your life. When it is complete, or can carry no more 'blessings', hang it on a wall as a reminder of the goodness the Universe showers upon you. If you decide to place the picture where visitors can see it this will doubtless entail having to explain what it is all about – another reminder of your blessings – maybe even resulting in your visitors creating their own 'Tree of Life'. This Exercise can also be a highly enjoyable project for children while they too learn to 'count their blessings'.

There is no limit to the amount of 'trees' you can prepare, just as there is no limit to the gifts of Universal Abundance.

URANUS

Forward, forward let us range, the ringing grooves of change.

Lord Tennyson 1809-1892

Colour: Turquoise. **Symbols:** Change and Freedom.
Energy: Yang. **Rules:** Aquarius. **Mode:** Fixed. **House:**
11th. **Time of Year:** January 20 - February 18. **Element:**
Air. **Chakra:** Brow (6th). **Cycle:** 84 years. **Stones:**
Aquamarine, Turquoise, Sapphire. **Metals:** Aluminium,
Chromium, Uranium.
Traditional Association: The Revolutionary.
Some Herbs and Flowers: Thyme, Celandine, Hops,
Jasmine, Magnolia, Meadowsweet, Passion flower,
Wintergreen, Orchid, Solomon's Seal. **Fruit:** Apples,
Kiwifruit, Elderberries.
Bach Flower Remedies: Rock Rose, Wild Oat, Walnut,
Star of Bethlehem.
Associated Words: Awake, Innovate, Higher Intelligence,
Paradox, Unusual, Original, Unpredictable, Abrupt,
Eccentric, Original, Progress, Community, Change, Future,
Grow, Independent, Rebel.

Uranus gets its name from Ouranos, the Greek word
for heaven. It is fourteen and a half times the size of earth,
has fifteen satellites, and was one of the last planets to be
discovered. Uranus has the most profound affect on
global changes.

The 'New Age' is not simply a nice 'hippy' idea of
everyone living together in peace and harmony – it is an

evolutionary shift in thought and belief. Changes now taking place, in both individuals and society, are inevitable. A virtual revolution is underway and Uranus energy is pushing us to accept the truths of existence by creating flashes of insight.

Very soon it will no longer be possible for even the most hardened sceptic to deny or resist the quantum changes forming at the very core of life. The sooner we accept that the present changes are for the best, the sooner humankind can get on with working towards a Higher goal. But for some this situation may create fear, fear will create resistance, resistance can develop into rebellion. There is little point in rebelling against what is happening, however, unless one can offer something better.

Take the teenage penchant for rebellion, for instance. When a young person first attempts to create a place in society he or she becomes aware of what is out of balance and decides to 'change the world'. Some join groups to work towards positive change while others become rebellious through craving 'freedom'. The teenage desire to actively push for 'freedom' is explosive and needs to be allowed safe expression unless it is to erupt into directionless havoc.

Uranian energy is unstoppable when it pulses through the body and can be experienced in two ways. Like the rebellious teenager it can burst from within or, if ignored, will swoop externally to force change upon us.

The more out-of-kilter we are to the 'spiritual revolution' the greater we will experience the negative force of Uranus. A difficult situation can be made more acute so it is no longer possible to ignore or avoid. In this case it is important to look closely at what is being shown and realign the Self with the Light. Trusting in your own spirituality will reveal the best way to react and resolve this situation.

Uranus also operates on another level. The more open, intuitive, and loving we are, the more this energy becomes a gift – a teacher who shines a light in the dark corners of life – as indicated by the Chakra associated with Uranus. The Third Eye or Brow Chakra is the eye of the soul, providing Divine insight to clarify our perception of the world and the purpose of life.

Bach Flower remedies assisting Uranus energy are: Rock Rose to increase the potential to overcome fear in a crisis and express the Higher Aspect in order to heal, grow, survive; Wild Oat helps decision-making in life direction and the expression of unique talents; Walnut is taken in the event of transformation and transition; Star of Bethlehem helps soothe the shock of enforced or sudden change.

Uranus has featured strongly in my life as one unexpected event followed another. While growing up I was affected when the family experienced many changes of mood, home, jobs, and interests. Then, after leaving home as a teenager, I moved around a good deal and tried different jobs as the rebellious energy inside fought to be free. For a time I lived in a peace camp protesting against nuclear arms which was, one might say, a highly Uranian way of life. We were woken daily by the police with garbage collectors who took our possessions for disposal. From one day to the next we never knew what was going to happen and lived with an ever-present expectation of danger. Existing outside the system, in that way, presented opportunities to be 'free' on some levels as there was no structure whatsoever to life – apart from the daily evictions of protesters. But the limits of no money, bad weather, ill health and constant fear, imposed greater restrictions than did the society we were attempting to change.

I came to realise that 'fighting' for peace was only adding more aggression to the world, not more peace; that I was perpetuating exactly what I was protesting against; that the first step towards getting to the root of human struggle has to be internal, within the Self. Instead I began to use my 'warrior spirit' to strive for spiritual growth and soon realised I had been so focused on the fear of annihilation that I forgot to notice the everyday miracles of Creation such as a tree, new life, a sunset or rainbow. I decided someone had to be happy and it might as well be me. What a pleasant surprise it was to find when I finally let go of fear and suffering they were quickly replaced with the Uranian energy of love and illumination.

Once we realise the Creative Force comes from within it changes, forever, the way we think and live. Since the Piscean Age, when Jesus was on Earth, a large proportion of humankind has been taught this Force belongs only to God and comes from Him, to us, through His various religious agents. This misinterpretation of the Word has led to a sense of isolation and separateness from the Source of Creation while building a considerable power structure for the Christian hierarchy. Constantly being reminded of natural human imperfections has weakened the individual to a point where he or she has become dependent on external spiritual agencies for help towards salvation.

Life, for most people, is a constant struggle between good and bad, right and wrong. This sort of 'black and white' reasoning creates duality – the 'I'm right so you must be wrong' kind of thinking. Many good souls are painfully torn apart through trying to do the best thing.

Now, as the new Age of Aquarius comes into being, a spiritual 'revolution' of global proportions is under way. Uranian energy, through change and freedom, is showing humankind there is another way to think – the cyclical way. We are learning there are no absolutes; everything in life is part of everything else; 'black and white' thinking is destructive; rigidity serves no useful or constructive purpose; life cannot be separated into compartments.

Understanding true spirituality means we understand God is within each of us rather than some remote force operating from 'out there somewhere'.

Supposing we question the popular image of an aloof Almighty? Is he a huge white-bearded old man who is perfectly contented to spend eternity watching for our failings, sitting in judgement, meting out punishment, willy-nilly, to guilty and innocent alike? Little wonder people turn away from this interpretation of God.

What is actually happening is that we are encouraged to seek perfection while denying our normal human imperfections. An extreme example is seen in those who desire 'world perfection' as they degenerate into the horrors of Fascism. This example of dualistic thinking illustrates the suffering one person or race can inflict on another in the name of 'perfection' or 'purity'. Accepting that imperfections are a legitimate part of our being, vital to the overall balance, is a positive leap towards the highest spiritual awareness through the Source of All Love.

'There is so much good in the worst of us,
And so much bad in the best of us,
That it hardly becomes any of us
To talk about the rest of us.'
Anon.

THE URANUS RITUAL

Although many people feel personally helpless in the face of all the suffering around our planet, everyone can help in some way. Remember, it is the single action of the individual that instigates change towards creating a better world. Anything from joining a human rights or environmental group to nursing the sick at home, volunteering to work in a war or famine-stricken area, becoming an alternative therapist, working as a psychic channel, or donating to charity, makes a difference to somebody else.

By volunteering, through this Ritual, to help others on a spiritual level your intention will be used by the Divine Power for the greater good of all. It need only be done once in a lifetime although an occasional reminder, by way of affirmation, will help re-focus your intentions.

Prepare your chosen area with blue candles and, if you wish, dab the pulse points on your wrists with sharp clean-smelling oil of Wintergreen to enhance your senses. Sit comfortably and prepare, as with the other Rituals, by asking for Protection and breathing deeply for a few moments. Concentrate to experience an intense awareness of the suffering that exists. If the need to cry arises take time to do so before continuing the Ritual.

Take your attention to your own situation and meditate on how lucky you are in comparison. Allow gratitude to enfold you and, as it does, imagine that you are becoming lighter as you fill with compassion. Let this feeling grow until it permeates your body and the need to help others forms like an ache deep inside.

Envisage yourself in spirit surrounded by other loving enlightened spirits who are already assisting in positive change. They welcome you with delight. Perhaps some look like your Guides or Angels, a spiritual teacher as in Jesus Christ, Buddha, Mohammed, Jehovah, Abraham, Guru, favourite Saints, or whatever feels true for you.

Tell them that you are volunteering to assist in creating a loving world and ask that they direct you from now on. Listen to their guidance, resolve to have the courage to carry out these directions and, rest assured, even if you cannot hear actual words the messages will come through your Higher instincts at some later stage. Be still and allow their love to cleanse you.

From this moment on you are part of the overall healing process and your life, if lived through love, will continually contribute to the Greater Good. Uranus will supply insight on how to grow and change and you will be assisted in every way by the Light but do not expect your life to be made easier overnight. That is up to you.

Return to your normal state of being when you feel ready. No need to take leave of your spiritual companions for they are always with you. Move your body slowly, stretch gently, relax and rise to your feet. Make a cup of tea, gaze out the window at the sky, communicate with a pet or perform some other everyday act to allow time to adjust. Trust that all the goodness of the Universe is on your side forever.

THE URANUS EXERCISE

Here is an entertaining opportunity to design an ideal world. Uranus influences the ability to express individual uniqueness – a direct link with personal creativity – and now this gift can be used to examine your Highest aspirations.

Everyone, without exception, has creative ability. It may surface in speech, the arts, craftwork, in personality traits such as being adventurous or gregarious, or in workplace skills such as cooking, hairdressing or fashion design. Those who claim not to be creative have simply overlooked or failed to recognise their specific area of talent. Finding an outlet for creativity is as important for the soul as nourishing and exercising is for the physical body.

The following Exercise, formulated for a group, is guaranteed to stretch the creativity and inventiveness of the individuals while contributing to the best for all. As the Universe receives the essence of intention rather than specifics it follows that any conscious positive thought helps influence the balance towards good.

The object is to create a description of your ideal world in the finest detail. What could be changed to enhance freedom? How would the political system operate? The monetary system – shells, tokens or exchange? Society – community or family groups? Homes – furniture, food, fuel?   Education? Transport? Business? Work? Communication? Entertainment? And so on, into every detail of how each component of life in this Utopia will influence the other.

For instance, if there was a world without electricity how would everyone communicate? By mail? But there would be no postal service as we know it without electricity. Telephone? Sorry. Clothes? Sorry – no high-speed sewing machines. Dress in skins? Not enough animals – even if we were willing to kill them. Cotton? Unable to harvest or import enough to survive winter (with multiple layers) without electricity. And just think of the unemployment. Time to reconsider and begin again.

Perhaps it would be best to save this Exercise for long winter evenings – maybe the Uranian influenced period between January 20 and February 18 – when the fire is blazing, television is switched off, and everyone can enthusiastically get in on the act at leisure. The participating group of family or friends will certainly get to know each other better and, as an added bonus, might even end up inventing the greatest board game of all time. It is amazing how creative we can be when we try – with Uranian energy.

NEPTUNE

Look homeward, Angel, now, and melt with ruth.

John Milton (1608-1674)

Colours: Sea green/ Blue. **Symbol:** Dissolve. **Energy:** Yin. **Rules:** Pisces. **Mode:** Mutable. **House:** 12th. **Time of Year:** February 19 - March 19. **Element:** Water. **Chakra:** Crown (7th). **Cycle:** 165 years. **Stones:** Tourmaline, Jade, Smoky Quartz. **Metal:** Platinum.

Traditional Association: The Sea.

Some Herbs and Flowers: Aloe Vera, Rosewood, Golden Seal, Hemp. **Vegetables:** Seaweed, Pumpkin, Chicory. **Fruit:** Lime, Melon.

Bach Flower Remedies: Mimulus, Aspen, Clematis, Wild Rose.

Associated Words: Surrender, Illusion, Invisible, Limitless, Intangible, Fog, Music, Soul, Spirituality, Subtle, Ideal, Compassion, Illusion, Fantasy, Fairies, Addiction, Merge, Ideal, Unity, Confusion.

Neptune is the gaseous non-identical twin of Uranus and has a core of rock. It is outermost of the giant planets.

When Neptune was discovered, in 1846, Western culture was first being introduced on a large scale to Eastern spiritual practises including meditation and yoga. These have since become widely accepted as important components in spiritual growth. Such teaching opens us to other ways of thinking and we now realise that surrender does not mean weakness but instead is a sign of great strength. Through courageously allowing old beliefs to dissolve and surrendering to the Divine it is possible for humans to progress and begin to understand the true meaning of Bliss.

Faith and surrender are the essence of Neptune energy, the dissolving force that brings all things together, merging physical, intellectual and spiritual life.

Western society, as a whole, is not educated to this way of thinking and many people are likely to feel threatened in the struggle to comprehend the nature of spirituality. Lack of understanding generates fear which is often numbed or distracted through addiction.

Society condones 'acceptable' addictions such as overwork, excessive accumulation of material possessions, relationships based in dependence, excessive alcohol intake, prescription drugs, gambling, and other panaceas. Addiction to illegal drugs or crime is a less socially acceptable extension of the need to distract. This negative aspect of Neptune's energy brings to mind the Sirens whose song lured the crew of Ulysses' boat onto the rocks of destruction. The further we travel from the Universal Truth the more difficult life becomes.

When we realise what spirituality means and strive to become one with it, the unknown waters of Neptune are infinitely more likely to carry our boat to a safe port rather than to drown us. Accepting Divine reasons for physical existence makes it a great deal easier to stay afloat through life's danger areas.

Mid-life crisis coincides with Neptune's Astrological activity. When this happens astute men and women quickly realise they may not know themselves as well as they thought. Life goes through a series of changes as previously familiar structures break down and dissolve. At the beginning most people attempt to hold on grimly, hoping it will pass, while nature, in conjunction with Neptune's energy, encourages using this important opportunity to surrender and evaluate life on all levels.

Surrender does not mean dissolving into an undefined cosmic blob but instead focuses on connecting with the Spirit. It also means letting go of past fears, fantasies and illusions, to go forward into the next phase of life with love and trust.

The Bach Flower Remedies for Neptune are: Mimulus to help overcome fears, particularily that of loss; Aspen for undefined fears; Clematis breaks the spell of illusion and escapism; Wild Rose gives a new sense of inner freedom and liberation.

THE NEPTUNE RITUAL

Long ago, before books were available, information was passed on through storytelling. Life was explained through archetypes in fairytales, myths and legends, where the truth was either exaggerated or simplified to get the message across. In this Ritual I have taken an image of the mermaid to represent mystical Neptunian properties. She will take us deep into ourselves to explore our fantasies, desires, and illusions.

This is best done in or near water. If a visit to sea, river, or lake is not possible a warm bath of water without additions will suffice. Water is the closest physical reminder of the spiritual in that it is clear, flowing, pure, natural, and part of the Whole.

Ask for protection and close your eyes. Relax and breathe deeply, Visualise a lovely mermaid, sitting on a rock opposite, smiling at you. She holds out a light but strong platinum cord which you take and tie securely to a nearby tree or rock. She is holding the other end and you can see it is very long.

As you slip into the warm water beside her you feel light and buoyant. With a strong flick of her tail she takes you deep into the water where you have no trouble breathing, seeing, or keeping up with her. You notice the surrounding beauty of water plants, anemones, coral, brightly coloured fish, and soft flowing music. This is a wonderful place and you would like to stay to enjoy its pleasures but she continues past, beckoning you to follow, as she trails the cord through it.

You continue until you come upon a giant mirror lying against a rock. It is perfectly framed with fabulous multi-coloured shells. The mermaid takes you in front of it and you see your reflection.

You look in wonder as your image becomes more perfect than it has ever been. It glows with health and beauty and all imperfections have disappeared. You want to stay but she urges you to move on. Notice the cord draped across the mirror as you go.

Further along you see an object lying on the sea bed. It is something you have recently desired – perhaps an item of clothing, jewellery or a book. Then you realise the sand is strewn with all the objects you have ever wanted but could not have. As you pause to gather them the mermaid beckons you to follow as she moves ahead, leaving a trail of cord across the area.

In the distance there is a strong white light and you swim together towards it. When you get closer it becomes so bright that you are almost unable to look at it, yet resist shielding your eyes for fear of losing sight of your mermaid guide. She senses your uncertainty, takes your hand, and leads you forwards.

As you swim nearer you begin to feel a deep sense of peace and love. On you go. Just as the light is getting too bright to bear you become aware of an exquisite Presence that is neither male nor female. This Being is very familiar, as if you have known each other all your life. And now, even though fully aware of all your strengths and weaknesses, the Being continues to radiate total accepting love towards you.

You know without doubt this Divine connection is all you have ever wanted and is all that is real. Your heart is wide open in a complete state of Trust and Surrender. No words are needed, no questions asked. Everything you could ever want is here in this moment.

You watch as the mermaid hands the end of your platinum cord to the Divinity and see it instantly transformed into a large transparent tube. The Being explains that whenever you feel lost, confused, disillusioned or overwhelmed with desire, you can use this route to swiftly connect with the Source of Unconditional Love.

As you step into the tube you feel the Being's gift of Love filling you to capacity and, after bidding the mermaid farewell, return alone along the same route at your own pace.

When you return, peacefully illuminated, to your

physical location, take time to contemplate. Accept that all previous desires and illusions mask a deep longing for Unconditional Love. You have now established this safe and unbreakable link with the Source, you alone have access to the tube and only you know the path through your imagination to the Centre.

Use the tube at any time to return to the Being when you feel the need for Unconditional Love and, if it ever feels blocked by fears or distractions, ask the Divinity to dissolve all obstacles by sending pure white spiritual light through it .

THE NEPTUNE EXERCISE

Water, the element that cleanses, purifies and sustains life, also soothes the troubled soul. It is impossible to walk by a seashore, stream, river or waterfall without feeling reassured by the benign presence of Mother Nature. Yet humanity is moving further away from everyday contact with water in its natural state. The water we drink comes from taps and plastic bottles, the water that cleans us comes through pipes and shower nozzles and we immerse our bodies in chemical-laden pools. When it rains we disappear indoors or shelter under umbrellas as if in sheer terror this wet stuff touch us and 'ruin' clothes, hair or makeup.

Why not, sample the invigorating pleasure of a real heavenly downpour on the next warm wet summer's day? This Exercise is simply to race outside into this natural shower and let yourself get soaked to the skin. If you can persuade friends to join you, all the better. It is important to wear something from your everyday summer wardrobe, like a T-shirt and shorts or cotton dress, to remind yourself this is a different to a shower or swim.

Get wet, get muddy, get happy, as you surrender to the element. Your clothes, like you, will wash clean. Remember what it was like to enjoy this simple fun as a child? Sing, dance, and jump around to let go of care and wash your worries away – before giggling your way indoors and leaping into a waiting hot bath or shower to dispel the vaguest possiblity of catching a chill. You cannot help but feel better afterwards.

PLUTO

Sleep after toil, port after stormy seas,
Ease after war, death after life doth greatly please.
Edmund Spencer (1552-1599)

Colours: Maroon/Black. **Symbol:** Letting Go.
Energy: Yin. **Rules:** Scorpio. **Mode:** Fixed. **House:** 8th.
Time of Year: October 22 - November 20.
Element: Water. **Chakras:** Sacral (2nd)/Crown (1st).
Cycle: 248 years. **Stone:** Opal. **Metals:** Steel, Plutonium.
Traditional Associations: Death and Rebirth.
Some Herbs and Flowers: Jasmine, Tulip, Rhododendron, Witch Hazel, Bottlebrush, Deadly Nightshade, Ivy, Geranium. **Vegetable:** Pumpkin.
Bach Flower Remedies: Olive, Mustard, Chestnut Bud, Walnut, Vine.
Associated Words: Transform, Regenerate, Intense, Taboo, Obsess, Deep Mystery, Control, Abuse of Power, Manipulation, Crisis, Sexuality, Incest, Birth, Terror, Shadow, Subconscious, Eliminate, Fate.

Pluto, furthest known planet from the Sun, is also the second smallest and believed to be made of ice. It represents birth, death, and rebirth in spiritual transformation as much as of the physical body.

The Chakras associated with Pluto are the Sacral, located in the area of reproduction, where creation takes place, and the Crown, where we connect with the Source and our destiny.

Opportunities occur frequently by which to learn, adapt and evolve, but there are some things we cannot change and Pluto represents this inevitable force. It is at once Creation and Destruction and its cycles are that of nature. Pluto energy offers no compromise and bows to no one. Physical death is one example of the inevitability of this planet's influence – as are such inescapable facts of life as loss, destruction and decay.

While Pluto's action cannot be stopped we can, with free will, choose how we react to it. Guided understanding shows us how and why such cycles occur and helps us to accept what we are unable to change. Those who deny the spiritual aspect of existence – the very reason we are on Earth – may find fear of pain and death inhibiting enjoyment of a full and active life. This negative way of relating to Pluto's influence is strongly supported by society's obsession with tragedy and disaster. The media, by dramatically reporting such occurrences on a daily basis, are catering to and intensifying this unhealthy interest.

Physical death is a frightening subject for us for several reasons. Over the last century it has gradually become a taboo subject and today death is virtually hidden from view in more sophisticated areas of the Western world except for horror films, violent videos and other forms of 'entertainment' designed to shock. Our society has strayed far from the Truth.

When death was openly accepted as part of natural existence humankind had respectful customs and ceremonies to help the bereaved of all cultures come to terms with a loss over a period of time. Today's method of dealing swiftly with death and burial in order to 'get on with everyday life' is a practical and sometimes callous denial of the Spirit. We are not a body with a soul but rather a soul with a body. There is no death of the soul. In coming to terms with and accepting the Truth we learn there is nothing to fear from physical death and that it is only another part of the cycle of life that can re-occur many times for each soul.

One of my first experiences of discovering how the power of the Spirit overshadows the frailty of physical life was through meeting a special woman when out with my mother. As we were introduced the elderly woman shook my hand and I will never forget the energy that emanated from her. It was as if she were pulling my soul further into my body. I could still feel her energy throbbing in my arm hours later.

My mother told me the woman was a Buddhist and they knew each other through a meditation group. When the woman died, soon after, an advanced Tibetan Lama who was visiting the area spent a week with her body, chanting and praying, to assist her soul to return to the Light. It was then I was told she was considered to be so highly evolved as to no longer require earthly incarnations and was ready to move on to a Higher Plane.

Simply shaking this woman's hand strengthened my spirit and although she was dying she had more power than anyone else I had ever touched. This incident made me realise that death is a beginning, not an end, and I'll never forget the gift she gave me.

The Bach Flower Remedies for Pluto are: Olive to re-establish peace after a long period of illness or stress;

Mustard lifts and lightens the mood; Chestnut Bud breaks cycles of attracting negative situations; Walnut assists with transformation; Vine helps let go of over-control.

THE PLUTO RITUAL

This addresses the process of Letting Go, which takes practise. The ultimate act of letting go in this existence is through our own death. When the actual event occurs it will be a great deal easier to accept if we can focus on Love and the Light rather than on fear and darkness.

While it is commonplace for mothers-to-be to practise the ritual of giving birth, it is virtually unheard of for anyone to practise a ritual for dying. By practising the Pluto Ritual we can at least address this natural occurrence until the idea that it awaits all of us becomes comfortably familiar rather than morbid.

Take one full day in bed. Sounds good? Do not be surprised to find this may be one of the more difficult things you have done for a while. We become trained for action at an early age and the very idea of going to bed without being sick, exhausted or depressed, brings out all sorts of excuses. But this is no ordinary day in bed and some forward planning is required.

You will need total, undisturbed, seclusion. The idea is not so much to escape reality as to absorb it. Get all nagging chores out of the way beforehand as you will need to give this healing Ritual full attention.

Resolve to abstain from, or at least curtail, the use of all addictive substances for the duration as a further commitment to letting go of destructive habits which can cloud the living years with pain and disease.

Gather a day's supply of light food and liquids such as water and fruit juice, brown rice cooked the previous day, a variety of fresh fruit and raw vegetables. Change your bed linen and air the room (not your usual bedroom if possible). Perhaps you might like to prepare by placing flowers, incense, a scented oil burner or candles around the bed. Remove the television, radio, newspapers, and any inappropriate books or magazines.

Begin the day with a bath or shower followed by a light breakfast from your supplies. Practise yoga or some stretching exercises before climbing into bed. Lie back comfortably and take a few deep breaths. Starting at the feet, work through your body to clench each voluntary muscle for the count of three, release and relax.

Now you can do any of the following while keeping in mind that the idea is to practise letting go, to slow down, develop trust, and enjoy not taking action. Repeat any of these several times if you wish and add whatever else might be appropriate.

Imagine you are falling from a great height and continue until you feel held and supported by reality.

Visualise yourself standing on top of a huge cliff. Look down at the sea crashing below and let yourself fall.

Think about what would happen to people you love if you were to leave the Earth today.

Consider the state of your life. Are you ready to go?

Supposing you were only allowed twelve companions. Who would you choose and why?

Imagine you were only allowed one possession from now on – what would you choose and why?

If you had your life to live over what would you

change?

Practise the Venus or Neptune Ritual.

Sleep if you need to.

Focus on your breathing and work on techniques for bringing the Light into your life.

Read inspirational books on healing, art, poetry, or other topics.

Look at your entire photograph collection and allow yourself to love and let go of the people, pets and places in them that belong in the past.

List all personality traits, characteristics and habits, that may be no longer working for you or are inappropriate to your life now. Let them go.

Think of how you have previously completed contact with people and places. Was the completion satisfactory to all parties concerned? How might it have been improved? Are you holding regrets? If so, let them go with love.

List all the 'bad habits' you have let go since childhood. How has this influenced you into becoming the person you are at this very moment?

There is no way of knowing what this Ritual will evoke for the individual until it is practised. You may feel bored, happy, frustrated, elated, lonely, peaceful, uneasy, or just physically uncomfortable. All of these discomforts are symptoms of resistance and will pass if you continue to let go.

End the Ritual at sunset/twilight with another shower or bath. Burn sage to clean the room and take a leisurely walk outdoors. Notice the beauty that surrounds you and thank your God for leaving you here to enjoy it.

THE PLUTO EXERCISE

In times of change we are left with a gap when the old has gone and the new has not yet settled into place. I refer to this 'gap' as the Void and our attitude when it occurs is of vital importance. This is what affects the ability to move on to better things. When confronted with a Void we can instinctively be moved by fear to fill it rather than pausing to allow inner change to develop.

Imagine that you are a field in which, each year, a crop is sown, grows and is harvested. This natural process is determined by the seasons. When Pluto is active you may feel empty and non-productive as if the crop has been harvested and you are lying fallow. You long to grow strawberries or daffodils, cabbages or corn; for children to play in your field; for animals, birds, butterflies and insects to live and thrive on your abundance. But it is winter and all is still.

Through recognising the cycle of nature we learn to accept and be at peace in the knowledge that the wheel will turn in time. This is the Void.

Eventually growth and movement begins again and you are unable to stop it. Even if no crop is sown in your field the soil will still sprout wild flowers and grasses once the rains fall and the sun shines upon it. These plants, in turn, attract insects and birds, people are drawn to this beautiful wilderness and so the cycle begins again.

The Void is an important period between Death and Rebirth in all aspects of life. It is a gift of time in which to rest. Think about times when there was 'nothing happening' for you and how the direction of your life might have taken a different turn once the Void was filled. Next time you experience this do not be afraid but rather take time to reflect and give thanks, knowing that new life is guaranteed when nature chooses it to begin.

SOARING HOME

For I dipt into the future, far as human eye could see,
Saw the Vision of the world, and all the wonders that would be.

Alfred, Lord Tennyson (1809-1892)

And so, this flight through the planets draws to an end as the Raven comes to roost once again on Mother Earth.

I trust the Astrological information helps to clarify some of the reasons we behave as we do and empowers you to work effortlessly with natural planetary influences by contributing to your understanding of them.

Sometimes we are inclined to carry too much responsibility for that which we cannot control and needlessly blame ourselves for unsatisfactory results. It helps to accept there is a Universal Plan at work, over all, every hour of every day. Goodness from the Source is not switched on and off at will and neither can humankind expect to achieve Enlightenment as a single blinding flash in this life or the next. It is only by striving to live every moment attuned to the Higher Self, practising love through respect, consideration, and compassion, that we can hope to even begin to understand the true concept of Enlightenment.

I hope you enjoyed, and benefited from, practising the various Rituals and Exercises and have fun now and in the future using the colours, gemstones, metals, fruit, flowers and fragrances, in whatever way feels appropriate.

The list of associated words included at the beginning of each chapter will help you to recognise and define a mood within yourself and the planetary influence which is responsible. For instance, you may have been surprised or unsettled, while reading this book, to discover yourself behaving exactly as nature intended.

This could simply have manifested in such ways as sleeping more (or less) than usual, having a 'chance' meeting with someone, experiencing a surge of energy/ joy/anger/ 'for no reason', or even struggling to ignore a feeling that there might be more to 'it all' than what you are presently experiencing. Now you know why!

Throughout life I have explored many dimensions of what it means to be human. The greatest discovery was Spirituality. At one time nothing in life made sense and I searched high and low to locate a truth that would tie the threads together. I did not find it until daring to admit I could not survive completely on my own. It was such a relief to discover the great spiritual 'network' of support.

The concept of life being a series of lessons, created to lead us back to the Light through full consciousness is, to me, the only sensible conclusion. We come into this life in innocence – surely we are not meant to leave it in ignorance?

Self-transformation is crucial as we move into, and become part of, the New Age. Through exploration of the astral, psychic, physical, emotional, intellectual and spiritual planes I learned everything, from colour to granite, is composed of vibrating energy and that this energy is influenced by how we think. Thoughts are also composed of this same vibrating energy. Negative thoughts, ideas, and beliefs drop the vibration to a slower frequency, which, in turn, attract intensely dense or negative experiences. Positive thought raises it in the same way and because Unconditional Love from the Divine vibrates at the highest frequency it is to this Source we need to direct our aspirations. Every single thought adds to the collective consciousness so, for this reason, we can help each other and Planet Earth by thinking positive loving thoughts. Simplicity is the key to understanding.

There are many Avatars, teachers, healers, counsellors, books and spiritual development groups available to help and inform. It is merely a case of choosing the method which is right for you. Trust your instincts.

Chari, my spiritual teacher, provides continuous guidance in my life and I have learned enough to know this personal journey to the Source, through Enlightenment, may continue over many future lifetimes.

Even the smallest change enhances life the very moment it is put into positive action but ultimately it is up to the individual to instigate spiritual growth. If it were not for the changes brought about by the 'chance' landing of a particularily wild raven on a little girl's shoulder, lifting her face (and focus) from ground to sky, it is unlikely I would be talking to you like this today. Perhaps you too will choose to continue the spiritual journey in your own way, in your own time, with Love.

RECOMMENDED READING

A Call to the Light Workers. Rhea Powers. Germany: Kumara Ass., 1990.

Astrology for the New Age. Marcus Allen. California: CRCS Publications, 1979.

Astrology and Spiritual Development. Donna Cunningham. California: Cassandra Press, 1989.

Body-Centred Psychotherapy. Ron Kurtz. California: Life Rhythm, 1990.

The Celestine Prophecy. James Redfield. Bantam Books, 1994.

Creative Astrology. Edited by Prudence Jane. England: The Aquarian Press, 1991.

Directory of Bach Flower Remedies. T. W. Heyne-Jones. England: Hillman Printers, 1976.

Emmanuel. Pat Rodegest & Judith Stanton. New York: Bantam Books, 1989.

Living in the Light. Shakti Gawain. California: Whatever Publishing, 1986.

My Master: The Essence of Pure Love. Shri P. Rajagopalachari. Shri Ram Chandra Mission, North America Publishing Committee, Pacific Grove, California, 1989.

The Motherpeace Tarot Playbook. Vicki Noble & Jonathan Tenney. California: Wingbow Press, 1986.

Opening to Channel. Sanaya Roman. California: H. J. Cramer Inc., 1987.

You Can Heal Your Life. Louise L. Hay. Santa Monica, California: Hay House, 1984.